YOUR DREAM.
GOD'S PLAN.

YOUR DREAM. GOD'S PLAN.

Are You Longing for Something More?

Tiffany Smiling
with Margot Starbuck

SHILOH RUN  PRESS
An Imprint of Barbour Publishing, Inc.

Print ISBN 978-1-68322-359-7

eBook Editions:
Adobe Digital Edition (.epub) 978-1-68322-535-5
Kindle and MobiPocket Edition (.prc) 978-1-68322-536-2

The author is represented by and this book is published in association with the literary agency of WordServe Literary Group, Ltd., www.wordserveliterary.com.

Published by Shiloh Run Press, an imprint of Barbour Publishing, Inc., P.O. Box 719, Uhrichsville, Ohio 44683, www.shilohrunpress.com.

Our mission is to publish and distribute inspirational products offering exceptional value and biblical encouragement to the masses.

Member of the
Evangelical Christian
Publishers Association

Printed in the United States of America.

CONTENTS

INTRODUCTION

Something Better Than Your Dreams

What girl doesn't want to live the story she's seen in the movies? Who doesn't want to be pursued by a soul mate and live happily ever after?

From the outside, my teenage life didn't look so very different from the glamorous lives of the leading ladies in the movies I'd seen. On my sixteenth birthday I looked out the window of our high-end home to see a brand-new-new black SUV in the driveway. My mom took care of my sister, my brother, and me; and my dad was a successful attorney. Our family vacationed at exclusive resorts in Maui and the Bahamas. At a glance, I was living the fairy tale.

But that picture didn't tell the whole story.

When I was ten years old, I was given a death sentence: three months to live. By God's grace I made it to sixteen when I literally exchanged an elegant ball gown for a worn cotton hospital gown, and a sparkling tiara for an MRI coil encircling my head. I was desperate to live a "normal" life, and with the help of my family and God, I fought my way back to *normal*, determined to live the dream on my heart.

But that didn't happen.

At the moment the "good life" was just within reach, I discovered that lasting satisfaction wasn't found where I thought it might be. In fact, as God revealed to me that scrambling after the dream I'd bought into would never satisfy, I tasted something even more fulfilling.

Hear me: I'm not knocking getting married, having a family, succeeding professionally, or even owning nice things. Rather, I'm observing that pouring our lives into the pursuit of our own happiness *has not served us well*.

Daily, we spend hours browsing others' happenings on social media. We work long hours to secure the next promotion or to pay for the clothes and car and house we believe will make us happy. We go to clubs with friends in the hope of real connection. But in our honest moments we realize that the happiness we've had has been fleeting.

Doing what advertisers and retailers and the media have conditioned us to do, scrambling to secure our own comfort and happiness, hasn't yet satisfied.

I'm sharing my story, of exchanging my dream for God's plan, with the hope that your eyes will be opened to the ways God is writing your own. Since the season I traded in my dream for God's plan, my life hasn't been the same. I've dashed with friends through a Guatemalan jungle to get a dying baby to a hospital. I've seen Ugandan orphans find family, food, and education. I've witnessed an entire Haitian village saved when they heard the Gospel of Jesus Christ for the first time. I've tasted life that leads to fulfillment and I want nothing more than for you to experience it too, tasting and seeing that the Lord is *good*. Trading in temporary for eternal, He is ready to raise up a generation who dares to believe that He will use them to change the world.

Beloved friends, Paul's words to first-century believers facing desperate times have never rung truer than they do today:

Don't waste your time on useless work,
mere busywork, the barren pursuits of dark-
ness. Expose these things for the sham they
are. It's a scandal when people waste their
lives on things they must do in the darkness
where no one will see. Rip the cover off
those frauds and see how attractive they
look in the light of Christ.

> *Wake up from your sleep,*
> *Climb out of your coffins;*
> *Christ will show you the light!*

So watch your step. Use your head. Make
the most of every chance you get. These are
desperate times! (Ephesians 5:11–16 MSG)

As you release the barren pursuit of earthly pleasures, exchanging it for the surprising way of Jesus, you will experience lasting satisfaction as you embrace what matters most.

—Tiffany Smiling

Chapter 1

THE DAY EVERYTHING CHANGES

*Because our time on this earth is fleeting,
every moment matters.*

"So how was it?" Jordan gushed as she got into my car, dropping her purse and bag in the backseat beside mine. "Your tan looks fabulous!"

Though I'd promised myself I wouldn't brag about the cruise, I couldn't keep a broad grin from exploding across my face.

I admitted, "It was awesome. Perfect weather most days and delicious food."

"Did you and Gentry find dresses today?" Jordan asked. She knew my sister and I had both been nominated for homecoming court and had looked for dresses in downtown Tulsa.

"We saw a few things we liked but didn't buy anything," I said. "We might try again this week. And if we have to go to Dallas next weekend, we can."

Jordan and I pulled into the restaurant parking lot to meet some of our guy friends right at six o'clock.

As I got out of the car, something felt *off* with my body. I couldn't quite place it, but I knew something wasn't right. It felt sort of like a pulse of energy, like before a sneeze, but it didn't itch and it didn't hurt. It just felt weird.

We walked thirty feet to the door, and as we entered we saw the guys in line. They were next up to order. Waving us over, they suggested we jump in and order ahead of them.

Stepping up to the counter, I told Jordan, "I don't feel good. . ."

Before she could ask for details, I started shaking. Without any control over my body, I fell forward, hitting my forehead on the restaurant's ceramic counter. The blow caused me to fall backward, knocking my head on the hard red tile floor.

Conscious and alert as it was happening, I knew I was having a massive seizure.

Jordan dropped to the floor, asking me what had just happened, but I was unable to tell her. The guys stood stunned. Though I'd known them all for years, none of them had ever seen me have a seizure.

My muscles tightened and my limbs seized with jerky motions. As my head hit the restaurant's red tile repeatedly, I could feel my brain shaking in my skull. And though my head was spinning and everything was becoming blurrier and blurrier, I was still aware of what was going on.

I tried to speak. In my head I was saying the words, "I'm having a seizure. Hold my head. Call 911. Call my mom."

But the sounds I heard passing through my lips weren't even intelligible. Awkward animal-like syllables gargled from my throat.

Incoherent utterances, "Ahh, agghh, ahh," were all that came out.

A crowd quickly gathered to watch the girl in the royal-blue dress lie on the floor convulsing. The store manager came over, children gawked, and a woman who'd been eating with her family, identifying herself as a nurse, bent down to protect my head.

As if at the end of a long, echoing tunnel, I heard

Jordan instructing, "Someone call 911!" I saw several people pick up their phones to make the call.

My vision and hearing continued to diminish. After about ninety seconds, I blacked out.

WHEN EVERYTHING CHANGES

Nurses were standing over me, taking my pulse and checking a fluid drip, when I awoke. Small engines whirred, and monitors beeped at regular intervals.

The first thing I remember is pain. I'd chipped my jawbone and had a concussion on the back of my head.

My mom was sitting by my bedside. Groggy from the drugs I'd been given, I could feel her hand on mine and hear her offering the nurse bits of my medical history.

"Tiffany has had cancer since she was ten. . . . She's been operated on three times. . . . Her last surgery was three years ago at St. Jude's. . . . She hasn't had a seizure since then. . . . No, she's not taking any medication now. . . ."

And although she didn't say it, I know my mom and I were both thinking the same thing: *we just returned from a cruise celebrating my full recovery yesterday.*

Even in my drugged haze, the irony wasn't lost on me.

I'd been given the Caribbean cruise by the Make-A-Wish Foundation several years earlier when I'd been too sick to use it. Because my seizures had stopped after my last surgery, we believed I was healthy. And all of my postoperative checkups had been full of good reports. My family had finally decided to take the cruise during the fall of my sophomore year in high school.

I glanced at the clock on the wall of my hospital room and, noticing a dark sky outside the single window beside my bed, realized it was eight at night. It seemed absurd to calculate that we'd been in Haiti two days earlier and had only docked in Miami the previous evening.

It was hard for me to process what was happening, and not just because of the sedatives. I knew my mom and I were both wrestling to piece together the disparate narrative, struggling to understand how our joyful celebration of life could have been so quickly extinguished.

Was it a mistake? Was this all just a really bad dream?

In all my wonderings, the one place I never let my mind go was death. I couldn't. I wouldn't.

What did upset me was that I'd finally regained some sense of equilibrium in my life. Because I had been seizure-free, I was gaining more independence. I'd just turned sixteen and been allowed to drive. I finally felt "normal." But the second I fell to the floor at Taco Bueno, I knew everything had changed. I understood that all the gains I'd made had been snatched away in that instant.

After the nurse left, my mom tilted her face toward mine. "Honey, your dad's on his way home. You just rest. We'll figure this out. God's got this."

I knew she was right, but we still didn't know what "this" was.

I closed my eyes and drifted out of consciousness once more.

MINUTES, HOURS, DAYS *MATTER*

When I was sixteen, I can't say that I'd lived the kind of life that would matter in eternity. Not surprisingly, my desires were like those of a lot of my peers: I wanted to look good when I went to school; I wore makeup and curled my hair. I appreciated an outfit that was put together well and had all the right designer labels. My family traveled often, and I had grown to love nice vacations. And the dream in my heart for my future looked similar to the life I was living.

Then suddenly, by circumstance, I became more keenly aware than many teenagers that our lives on this earth are fleeting. Although I tried to push the thought out of my mind, I realized I didn't know how many more birthdays I'd see. Life became fragile, and time became important. Every minute was a treasure.

Yet, although my circumstances were dire, I never feared death. I'd given my life to Jesus on Valentine's Day in kindergarten. He'd been an important part of my life since then, but now I became more aware of the gift I'd been given. As I felt the near grip of death, I began to realize, even more deeply, that He'd sacrificed His life so that I could live forever. He traded His death for my living.

The story we've been told since we were girls is that we'll be happy, or "full of life," when we project a certain image, earn more money, improve our social status, get our dream guy, own the house, have the kids, and grow our pile of possessions. It's what I believed, and maybe it's what you've believed, too. In themselves, those aren't bad dreams. When God offers them as gifts, we can receive them with grateful hearts.

But I've become more and more concerned about the ways our generation is using our time, money, and energy in *pursuit of our own dreams and desires*. To be fair, when we scramble after what we think will make us happy, we're doing exactly what we've been trained to do. Advertisers have promised that we'll be happy with a closet full of fabulous clothes. Social media promises that we'll feel fulfilled with a perfectly toned body, a beautiful family, and more "likes." Movies have promised we can find a flawless romance that will eliminate our insecurities. And yet, while the clothes, the guy, or the body might satisfy for a moment, dreams that fall short of God's plans leave us empty, hurting, broken, and lonely.

You were made for so much more. If you are a student or a single working woman or a missionary or a full-time mommy, there is a calling over your life that involves bringing light to the dark places—in university hallways, in work cubicles, in overseas villages, and in the rooms of your home. If you are willing to release your grip on the plans you've been holding for your life, God is waiting to show you His plan that is even better for you and for the people He loves.

Maybe my brush with death heightened my awareness of what matters most: the value of my time on this earth and the importance of living it to the full. Cancer or no cancer, though, each of us will find lasting satisfaction in the way we steward the years and days and minutes we've been given.

AN UNCERTAIN FUTURE

When I awoke again, it was late Friday evening. Nurses bustled in and out of my room. Monitors beeped, and I noticed an IV in my arm.

My mom was still sitting beside my bed, and she noticed my eyes flutter open.

"Hi, sweetheart," she said, smiling bravely.

"Hi, Mom," I answered, noticing how dry my mouth was.

She assured me, "Dad's flying home from Chicago now. And the nurses say you could be released this afternoon if they can get you in for an MRI this morning."

"And do they know what happened?" I asked.

But I knew the answer even as I was asking the question. My condition was so rare that even the most elite surgeons in the nation had only seen six or seven similar cases throughout their careers. I knew I'd need to return to St. Jude's Children's Hospital for diagnosis and treatment.

My mother said what I expected: "We'll have to go see Dr. Sanford."

Dr. Sanford, who practiced at St. Jude's, was the single surgeon who'd agreed to treat me after seeing my charts six years earlier. He'd last operated on me three years earlier. We trusted him completely.

"Can we wait until after homecoming?" I pleaded.

My mom explained, "You'll have an MRI, and then we'll see what Dr. Sanford says."

Though my mom kept a brave face, I heard the concern in her voice.

TIME MATTERS

Today, over a decade later, I remain more convinced than ever that every moment matters.

What about you? Do you believe you were made for a life that is really worth living? Are you convinced that God longs to use all of your experiences, passions, and gifts to accomplish His greater purpose—the very thing He created you to do? Maybe that "something more" your heart is longing for isn't clear right now. That's okay. As you offer yourself to God, as you release your life to Him, He will guide you to a life that's worth living.

The time we are living in is darker than we know; and

our time on this earth is more valuable than we know. And at this moment, God is sparking a fire within His people "to fulfill his good purpose" (Philippians 2:13). You are being prepared to serve and grow the kingdom in a specific way, using the unique gifts and passions and skills you've been given.

If you were raised in the US like I was, to dream of a comfortable future where all your needs and desires are met, the way of Jesus will seem radically different. It doesn't make sense in a culture where we're barraged daily by messages insisting that we deserve to be instantly satisfied. And yet I've learned firsthand that this unlikely way—the radically different way of Jesus—is the way to life that really is fulfilling.

GOWN AND CROWN

After Jordan had called my mom to meet us at the hospital, our family friend Dr. Reese, who happened to be on call at the hospital that evening jumped in to help. As a result, the staff had been ready to receive me before the ambulance had even arrived. Within an hour of my initial examination, I was being wheeled down the hallway toward radiology. I knew the route—the nurses' stations, waiting rooms, ceiling tiles—more intimately than I cared to. When we got to radiology, the transporter asked the technician if he should leave me in the waiting room or take me straight in. Per orders, he wheeled me right into the MRI room.

I knew the drill. The technician helped me slide over onto the MRI machine. After I lay down, she helped me settle into the best position. As I entered the machine, I knew to lie perfectly still and also to request the latest

Rascal Flatts soundtrack to drown out the loud noise of the medical machinery.

As I lay in the worn hospital gown, surrounded by a crown of medical coils, I closed my eyes and focused on a different kind of crown and gown: homecoming was just two weeks away.

CHAPTER 2

ST. JUDE'S, WISHES, AND ENRIQUE IGLESIAS

Expect trials on the journey.

"Celebrate her birthday big this year."

Those words from the head neurosurgeon at one of the nation's leading cancer hospitals, spoken to my parents after I'd been asked to leave the room, were polite code for a death sentence.

As I approached my eleventh birthday, he'd just given me ten months to live.

He also refused to operate. Because the tumor was touching my motor strip, which controls the voluntary movements of skeletal muscles, he believed there was a greater chance he could hurt me than help me.

My parents, who believed in a God who was bigger than a doctor's report, and who didn't want to alarm me, assured me we'd continue searching for the right treatment.

THE SPOT

In the spring of fourth grade I began noticing odd sensations on the left side of my body. A tingling would begin in my leg, sort of like that feeling when your hand or foot falls asleep. The sensation would climb up the side of my body and down my left arm, then all the way up to my face, causing numbness.

Concerned, my mom made an appointment with our pediatrician. He sent us to a local neurologist.

An MRI showed a small spot on the right side of my

brain, but doctors were unable to identify conclusively what it might be. It might be a tumor, they explained, but it could just as easily be a knotted blood vessel. Doctors just couldn't tell. Because they did identify the numbness I was experiencing to be small seizures, doctors put me on seizure medications and ordered an MRI every three months to monitor the irregularity. We also visited a doctor in Houston who determined that the "spot" over my right ear was lodged deep in the brain.

Deciding it was too risky to operate, the doctors decided to continue the quarterly MRIs.

I was completely embarrassed whenever I'd have seizures around others. As a quiet girl, very shy and reserved, I hated attention. And when these mini seizures would creep across my body, I wasn't able to speak. If I felt a seizure coming on when my friends and I were at a movie, I wouldn't dream of mentioning it. But when we'd be chatting at a slumber party, or hanging out together at the mall, it was harder to hide. I dreaded meeting my friends' eyes when they'd notice that I couldn't speak. When the seizure would pass and I could engage again, I tried to minimize it like it wasn't a big deal. But as a girl who wanted nothing more than to be normal, I'd always cringe a little on the inside.

Twenty months after the numbness began, an MRI revealed that the blood vessel we'd been watching was now leaking a small amount of blood. Now that I was at risk for an aneurysm, surgery was advised. But because there wasn't a pediatric neurosurgeon in Oklahoma in 2000, we decided to do our own research.

Disappointed but desperate, we did.

The attorney in my father's law firm who was responsible for securing medical records to prepare them for trial jumped in to help. He sent my MRIs to the top four neurosurgeons in the world. As we traveled across the country to meet these surgeons face-to-face, we always received the same response. Doctor after doctor turned us down. The dangerous surgery, they claimed, was just too risky. We appealed to doctors in the very best hospitals in the nation, but none were willing to operate. We even had an appointment scheduled with renowned Johns Hopkins neurosurgeon Ben Carson, but when he was diagnosed with his own cancer during that process, we weren't able to move forward.

Finally, a doctor agreed to take the risk to operate in an attempt to stop the leaking blood vessel in my brain. Dr. Robert Spetzler, at St. Joseph's Hospital in Phoenix, Arizona, specialized in cerebrovascular disease.

But even after we'd identified Dr. Spetzler, who agreed to treat me, we faced a maddening delay when our insurance company refused to refer the risky surgery, so I could not get admitted to the hospital.

Their decision wasn't one my father was willing to accept.

Just two days before Dr. Spetzler was scheduled to operate on me, my dad arranged a three-way call with Dr. Spetzler and our health insurance company.

When everyone had dialed in, my dad alerted all parties that the call was being recorded for his legal records.

Then he asked the world-renowned surgeon, "When I file a lawsuit against this company for refusing to let me get treatment for my dying daughter, Dr. Spetzler, will you testify as a witness?"

Dr. Spetzler said that he would, confirming, "This procedure is indispensable."

He had their attention.

If the insurance company had done their homework, and I suspect they had, they would have discovered that not only was my father a dad with a sick daughter, but over half of the companies on the list of clients his firm had represented were insurance companies. He was intimately familiar with insurance law, and his courtroom record spoke for itself. If he'd sued, he would have been a formidable opponent.

The surgery, the company finally conceded, would be covered.

At the time, I was pretty oblivious to my father's advocacy and all the different ways he would intervene on my behalf. When local doctors couldn't treat me, he never stopped fighting for me. But I later decided that what my dad did for me gave me a glimpse into the heart of my heavenly Father, who fights enemies we may never see.

There are times, though, when we *are* able to see these conflicts unfold with our own eyes. These battles—the diagnosis, the financial hardship, the broken heart—give us the opportunity to trust God and witness His work on our behalf. As our gracious and loving Father, the Lord shapes and strengthens our faith through these trials.

ONE WHO IS GREAT

Prior to my first surgery, my mom seized every opportunity to build my faith and strengthen her own.

Seriously. . .my mom was a gem.

During our morning family devotions, she'd remind me that nothing is too difficult for God. Each morning we sang a song about God's greatness and miracles a cappella. We'd even sing praise and worship songs along with our favorite CDs in the car on the way to school.

While I slept, my mom would kneel at the foot of my bed, offering me into God's hands. And even though I was sound asleep, her prayers became a familiar refrain that was knit into my deep places: "Lord, I place Tiffany in Your care. Her life is a gift from You, Lord. You know what's best. You know what lies ahead. I trust You. It's hard to understand that You could possibly love her more than I do, but You do."

What I never would have guessed, at age ten, or twelve, or fourteen, or even sixteen, was that when I went to school, my mom would break down in tears. I didn't learn this until years later. When I was around she always showed a brave face. And because my parents didn't want to worry me until they could give me reliable information about the procedure, I was mostly oblivious to what we were up against during those four grueling months of waiting.

In so many ways, our family's life was a contradiction. We were financially secure; we were poised; we were joyful; we loved each other. From the outside, it appeared that we had it all. But every day we fought and prayed, foot soldiers in a battle between life and death. My mom set the tone for our home by believing that, on the very best days and the very worst days, God was still God, and God deserved our praise.

And that's what God got: *our praise.*

One morning I awoke to see that my mom had taped a sheet of her monogrammed pink-and-green flowered stationery to my bathroom mirror, with these words penned in flowing cursive:

> *"So do not fear, for I am with you;*
> *do not be dismayed, for I am your God.*
> *I will strengthen you and help you;*
> *I will uphold you with my righteous right*
> *hand."* (Isaiah 41:10)

She taped another sheet announcing God's promise, in her familiar handwriting, to my nightstand: "I am the LORD, the God of all mankind. Is anything too hard for me?" (Jeremiah 32:27).

And on my dresser, I daily read of God's plan for my life: " 'I know the plans I have for you,' declares the LORD, 'plans to prosper you and not to harm you, plans to give you hope and a future' " (Jeremiah 29:11). That verse, pinned to my dresser, would become one of my favorites. When I most needed to know that God had a plan for my life, despite the battle I was facing, I'd call it to mind.

Because God has a purpose for our lives, there is purpose in our circumstances. Even though our futures are not known to us, God promises a beautiful future to those who trust Him. And while our circumstances don't always reflect God's perfect plan, they always provide opportunities to believe the truth of God's Word when we can't yet see it.

I confess, I didn't always understand the meaning of that verse my mom taught me from Jeremiah 29. In fact, I read it to mean that I could dream my own dreams for my life and expect the Lord to bless them with prosperity and the picture-perfect future I'd imagined.

Maybe you've found yourself in a similar place. We

chase our dreams—our pleasures and desires—and wonder why we aren't receiving the blessing the Lord promises. We pursue relationships, careers, and other personal gains. They might not be bad things, but if they're not a part of God's plan, they can leave us hurt and lonely, still hungering for God's blessing. God's intention was never that we would make our own plans for our lives; rather, God's Word through Jeremiah promises that there is already a plan He wants to reveal to you and to me.

Though faith isn't inherited the way dark hair or blue eyes might be, my parents' faith had shaped our home in such a way that I'd been given the opportunity to know and trust the Father of Jesus. Though it would be years before I would experience the kind of depth I saw in my mom's faith, and my dad's as well, I'd been gifted with a solid spiritual foundation.

That burgeoning faith is why in Phoenix, Arizona, on the morning of my first surgery when I was twelve years old, I was singing the song our family had sung so many times in the car on the way to school, "How Great Is Our God" by Chris Tomlin.

The procedure lasted three and a half hours. When Dr. Spetzler finished closing my skull, he went to the waiting room to speak to my parents. Though he'd been able to stop the bleeding on my brain, he'd discovered something more.

He'd found a tumor.

JOURNEYING FORWARD

My family waited three harrowing months for the pathology reports to provide the information we needed to move forward. Discovering the tumor meant we'd now need to search for the surgeon who'd be willing to risk removing it. But that person was hard to find.

Dr. Spetzler had sent us home with instructions to begin chemotherapy immediately. Later that week I was being fitted for a chemo helmet at a local hospital.

As we wound our way through the sterile hospital hallways on my way home, smelling the faint odor of antiseptic, my father ran into a doctor whom he'd once represented in court. When he explained to her why we were there, detailing my medical journey, I saw her face fall.

She pulled us into a quiet alcove to continue the conversation.

"Mark," she whispered, in case the walls had ears, "I cannot let you get chemo here."

I saw my dad's eyes widen.

"Because her tumor is such a rare, rare form, and because it's in such a dangerous area of the brain, you want to go to a hospital that specializes in rare pediatric cancers."

My dad explained, "We've tried every place and everyone. And we're being forced to make a fast decision."

His doctor friend continued to speak in hushed tones. "Don't tell anyone here. I'm going to refer you to St. Jude's. I used to work there and have an 'in' with the team of doctors there."

"In Memphis?" my dad asked. He was clarifying that she was referring to the famous St. Jude's Children's Hospital four hundred miles away from our home.

"Yes," the doctor confirmed. "Have Tiffany's reports sent to me tonight, and I'll send them to the team."

I'd already been missing a lot of school for local doctor's appointments, and now she wanted me to fly to Memphis for them?

My dad didn't even blink at the mention of treatment in Memphis. I had confidence that my parents would do whatever I needed to get well.

ST. JUDE'S

When Dr. Larry Kun, head of oncology at St. Jude's, studied the reports, he agreed to meet with us. Two days after we'd bumped into my dad's friend in the local hospital, my mom and dad and I flew to Memphis so that Dr. Kun could conduct a battery of tests that would map my brain to determine what damage could potentially result from removing the tumor several doctors had already refused to touch.

While most hospitals are typically drab and sterile, St. Jude's was different. Stepping through the front door, visitors are met with an explosion of color, not unlike the most spectacular children's museums. The walls, featuring a variety of artwork and displays, were painted in kid-friendly colors, and even the tiles on the floor were bright. Inside the entrance was a big basket of striped and sparkly beanies for children who'd lost their hair to chemotherapy or radiation. Some of the walls were tall, narrow fish tanks hosting a variety of species. In addition to a menu of the most nutritious foods for sick bodies, the cafeteria also had a sushi bar, an ice cream and cookie bar, and areas featuring food catered by local Memphis restaurants. There were days when therapy dogs visited and seemed to be on every floor of the building.

It was an amazing facility, but on that first visit for the tests Dr. Kun had ordered, I made it known that I didn't want to be associated with the other patients at St. Jude's. I don't mean I didn't want to befriend them, because we did meet some truly amazing children there. But many of them were very ill. Compromised. Vulnerable. They were pale. Some were thin. Many had lost their hair. Some had lost limbs. It was important for my own sense of identity to continue to believe that I was "other" than they were. I was *visiting*. I'd come to get a surgery, and then I'd go back home to my normal life. I was going to stay *normal*.

One week after that first visit, my mom and dad and I returned to St. Jude's to meet with Dr. Kun about what he'd discovered. He strongly encouraged us to meet with a St. Jude's neurosurgeon, Dr. Alex Sanford, to schedule surgery to remove the tumor.

Dr. Sanford began by reiterating what my parents had already discovered in their research: a child is the best person to operate on because of the malleability of the growing brain, and in my case the worst person to treat with chemotherapy, since the treatment has dangerous side effects for the kind of tumor that I had—including organ damage, vision impairment, and others.

I heard my dad breathe a sigh of relief.

Dr. Sanford then explained that there was something very unique about my tumor. A tumor is typically a different color than the brain tissue surrounding it. But in my case, the color of the tumor was identical to the surrounding tissue. And the scans were reading the scar tissue from my previous surgery as being part of the tumor. So my brain surgery would be performed by touch because brain tissue and cancer *feel* different.

Unlike all the specialists we'd sought out, Dr. Sanford was the only one who agreed to operate on my tumor.

"We can do this," he explained. I heard a confident kindness in his voice. "Yes, Tiffany's cancer is rare. And it's in a very delicate location, but this is what I do. It's my specialty."

My parents exchanged a glance that said more than words could have. They'd found our hero.

Though gifted and kind, Dr. Sanford was also realistic. He anticipated the possibility that I would experience weakness on my left side after the surgery.

I was determined, with Dr. Sanford's help, to have a normal childhood.

MAKE-A-WISH

After my first visit to St. Jude's, I'd been granted a wish trip from the Make-A-Wish foundation. Make-A-Wish grants the wishes of children diagnosed with a life-threatening medical condition. One child might want to swim with the whales. Another might want to record an original song. Another might want to throw the opening pitch at a baseball game. Another child might want to visit The Weather Channel. The organization believes that wish experiences can be game changers in the lives of children and families.

My wish was to meet recording artist Enrique Iglesias. My sister and I owned all of his songs and had all of them memorized. When I made my wish known, the organization went into action. Serendipitously, Iglesias had a concert scheduled in Tulsa two months later! It wasn't just that I was going to get to go to the concert. My sister, as well as our cousins Brooke and Brittany, were going to be picked up in a limousine, sit in the front row of the venue, and be invited backstage after the concert.

Basically, I was about to live out the fantasy of middle school girls everywhere.

The day of the concert, my mom picked me up from school early because the limo would pick us all up at our house.

When I was upstairs with Gentry getting ready, my mom received a call that the concert had been canceled. Enrique Iglesias was sick.

Not as sick as I was. . .but too sick to perform that night.

To say that I was bummed is a wild understatement.

And because I had to fly back to Memphis for surgery the next week, my wish had to be postponed.

SURGERY

Four days after the concert was canceled, my parents and I were back at St. Jude's.

We checked in the night before my surgery. The following morning the staff woke me up before 6:00 a.m. I chatted with my parents for a bit, prayed with them, and had an IV inserted in my arm. When the nurse administered medication in it, I drifted off to sleep.

Dr. Sanford operated successfully, confident he'd gotten all of the tumor. But we understood the routine. Scans would be performed; tissue would be sent to pathology. We'd monitor my post-surgery recovery. I'd return in three months for another scan.

The pathology report identified the growth as a pleomorphic xanthoastrocytoma (well-differentiated astrocytoma) brain tumor, a very rare nonmalignant tumor with two different families of tumors in one. St. Jude's had only ever seen this tumor in six to eight other children prior to my diagnosis.

Unfortunately, I continued to have two or three small tingly seizures each day. This concerned Dr. Sanford because if the tumor *had* been completely excised, the seizures should have stopped in time. Regular MRIs continued, and when we returned to St. Jude's about nine months later, Dr. Sanford noticed something suspicious.

Suspecting it was a bit of tumor he'd missed, he operated again two months later.

RISK

Dr. Sanford was in a difficult position.

The night before my third operation, Dr. Sanford stopped by my room to discuss the risks with my parents. He didn't want to go too deep and risk damaging good brain tissue on the motor strip. The tumor, he explained, was about the size of a quarter, but it was attached to a large blood vessel. If he damaged that vessel in any way, he warned, I could have permanent stroke damage. The chances of that, he explained, were about one in twenty.

I was only fourteen, but even I could do the ominous math.

After Dr. Sanford left the room, my parents and I shared prayer and devotions together. We sang the same song I'd sung before my first surgery, "How Great

Is Our God." Then my dad, exhausted, returned to the hotel to get some rest, and my mom pulled a blanket over her lap in a reclining chair next to my bed. She'd stay throughout the night.

Though I trusted God, I'd heard Dr. Sanford's cautions and I understood the gravity of what I was facing.

CONSCIOUSNESS

The procedure, which lasted almost five hours, was a success. The tumor had actually been attached to a smaller blood vessel and not the larger one Dr. Sanford had anticipated.

Around lunchtime I woke up to nurses gently pelting me with questions. Because Dr. Sanford had nicked the small blood vessel during surgery and stitched it back up, they wanted to rule out the possibility that I might have suffered a ministroke. So a sweet nurse with colorful SpongeBob scrubs was asking me to squeeze her left hand with my left one to confirm that I still had strength on both sides of my body. Though groggy, I passed with flying colors.

Within three months of returning home, I was healed of epilepsy. I was weaned off all the seizure medications I'd been taking, over 1000 milligrams a day, and I was finally seizure-free for the first time in four years. My family had a big party to celebrate with our friends and family.

Going into ninth grade at Jenks High School, I was healthy and happy. I enjoyed weekend sleepovers and pool parties with my girlfriends. Our high school prided itself on having one of the best football programs in the nation, and the games were the highlight of our weekend fun.

The summer before my sophomore year, Make-A-Wish contacted my mom, because I had never had the opportunity to reschedule my wish. In the wake of our post-surgery med-free celebration, the possibility of pursuing a wish felt a little different to me and a lot different to my parents. We'd no longer be making memories because my life might contain fewer days than most. Instead we'd be celebrating God's gracious provision that would allow me many more years of memories with family and loved ones.

By that point, I was over Enrique. So six weeks after my sixteenth birthday, in the fall of my sophomore year of high school, Make-A-Wish sent me and my family on a Caribbean cruise to celebrate my good health.

CHAPTER 3

THE DEVIL'S HAND

Satan attempts to thwart God's dream.

I suffered my seizure in Taco Bueno the day after we returned from our celebratory cruise to the Caribbean. Because we trusted in a loving and gracious God, we couldn't understand the absurd timing of what felt like a vicious attack by the enemy. Though Dr. Sanford had been confident he'd removed all of the tumor two years earlier, scans taken immediately after that humiliating seizure revealed that the tumor was still active.

The day of the seizure, Gentry and I, both on the homecoming court, had been shopping for dresses for homecoming. We had dresses for the dance but intended to wear different gowns for the football game homecoming court presentation. In what continued to be the oddest juxtaposition of joy and pain, normal and abnormal, the day after I was released from the hospital—knowing I'd most likely be back at St. Jude's for surgery in a matter of days or weeks—I went shopping and found the gown I'd wear at the homecoming game.

When my dad escorted me down the aisle at the football game, I looked like the teenage girl who has it all. And honestly, I did! By no merit of my own, I enjoyed a family that was highly admired, a closet full of clothes, a car in the driveway, supportive girlfriends, and an athletic boyfriend. And that chilly evening, as I paraded down the turf in a shimmering black gown, the crowd clapped and cheered and hooted as my name was announced in front of the whole high school.

In that glorious moment, I pushed away the lurking knowledge that I'd soon be back at St. Jude's.

GAME PLAN

Maybe you've heard stories of children born with disabilities that require surgeries throughout childhood to accommodate their growth. Or maybe you've heard of someone in a terrible car or biking accident who required surgery after surgery to piece their body back together. With the advance of medical technology in the last twenty years, we often assume that if we just keep operating, or just keep medicating, victory is certain.

But of course, we know that's not always true. Patients are disabled when surgeries go awry. Chemotherapies fail. Uncontrollable infections set in. And teenage girls die from brain tumors. My family had faced that terrifying possibility years earlier.

Three weeks after returning from our cruise celebrating my full recovery, we'd checked back in to St. Jude's. The contrast between life and death was stark. The afternoon before what would be my fourth surgery, Dr. Sanford visited us in my room. Both of my parents were at my side.

"Hi, Tiffany." Dr. Sanford greeted me warmly, as if our relationship was that of a teacher and his favorite student.

He shook my parents' hands and greeted them, too.

We chatted about homecoming and then his expression turned serious.

"You know that each time I open her up she's at risk." Somber, he added, "I wouldn't be doing my job if I didn't tell you."

My parents nodded solemnly. They knew there was the risk of infection or complication that's inherent in any surgery. But because my cancer was in my brain and my tumor was situated on my motor cortex, the risk was even greater. Every surgery left scar tissue, which made accessing the tumor more difficult the following time. We understood the risks.

"This is going to be our last surgery," he said solemnly. "It just won't be safe to operate again, and this is our last chance to get the entire tumor."

My mother pressed her lips together as she received his words.

"I'll be as aggressive as I can be, and I hope to get it all."

He continued to describe the procedure and the risks, but most of the words bounced off my ears. It was too much to take in.

Before he left, we all thanked him politely for the horrible news.

THE BIG DAY

The next morning, one of the nurses came in to shave my head. As you might imagine, this was a pretty huge deal for a sixteen-year-old girl. Because I'd fought to save as much hair as possible, they agreed not to shave my entire scalp. That made for a fairly elaborate process. Carefully parting my hair and clipping sections of it back, the nurse shaved a two-inch strip from my ear to the top of my head. Across the rest of my scalp she shaved small areas where monitors would be attached.

When the nurse finished, I raised my hand to feel the smooth skin where she'd shaved the largest strip. I gently touched the area closest to my ear but couldn't bear to feel more. When she offered to bring a mirror so I could see her handiwork, I refused.

My parents were right by my side as I was wheeled down the hallway to surgery. We had prayed together and sung "How Great Is Our God," and now they were releasing me to the surgeon who was committed to helping me.

UNCLE DARRYL

About three hours into the surgery, my dad's brother-in-law, my uncle Darryl, called to speak to my parents.

My uncle Darryl was one of the thousands of people around the world who rallied around our family in prayer during each brain surgery. Each time, people in various cities and states and countries, many we'd never even met, took turns praying day and night, even taking time off of work to pray on our behalf.

Darryl had been praying earlier that day for my procedure. He had gone to work in the morning and was scheduled for an afternoon meeting, but he left before noon to go home and pray for me, because God gave him a vision that gripped his heart.

That day my uncle wrestled in prayer for me. He also struggled to know whether he was meant to share with us what had been revealed to him. God prompted him to call my parents.

Uncle Darryl began, "The Lord showed me that the devil's hand is trying to get control of Tiffany's life. . . her brain."

My dad was silent. What could he say? The vision my uncle had received wasn't exactly the kind one hopes for.

My uncle explained a bit more of what the Lord had shown him in prayer. He'd seen an image of the devil's hand grasping at my brain.

"Well, that may be, but our God is more powerful than the enemy," my dad insisted. "We'll keep praying, and you keep praying."

About thirty minutes later, Dr. Sanford, sweating and shaking his hands as he walked, came to the waiting room and sat down beside my parents.

"This is going to take longer than we'd anticipated," he explained.

"Why is that?" my mom asked, concerned.

"The tumor," he reported, "is in the shape of an elongated hand." He held out his hand to show her. "It has fingerlike tentacles that are gripping the brain tissue. Releasing each of those is just going to take more time."

Wide-eyed, recalling my uncle's vision, my parents glanced at one another.

"Thank you, Doctor," my dad somberly replied, patting the doctor on the back.

Dr. Sanford disappeared back through the double doors leading to the operating room.

My parents continued to pray that the devil's hand would not prevail. . .that God would empower and guide Dr. Sanford's hands. They knew that any hope for a future rested in the hands of the One who made me.

Four hours after that first report, the doctor reappeared. His expression was grim.

This time my father wrapped his arm around my mother.

Without the formality of a greeting, he simply explained, "When I was releasing the tumor from the healthy brain tissue, I nicked one of Tiffany's blood vessels."

My dad gripped my mom tighter.

"The bleeding is under control now," the doctor explained, "but there's the possibility that Tiffany has suffered a stroke. We won't know until she wakes up. I'm going to get back in there now."

As he returned to the operating room, both of my parents sank into the sofa in the waiting room and wept.

At 10:30 that evening, Dr. Sanford, who'd completed the surgery, came to deliver his final report.

My parents wearily stood when they saw him approach.

"Well," he said, looking much more relaxed than he had all day, "I think we got it all."

My parents exhaled.

"We're just going to have to see how she responds when she wakes up."

POST-SURGERY

Waking up was a slow process. The surgical team had put me in a medically induced coma to allow my brain to rest after the trauma of surgery.

My parents were watching over me when I finally woke up in the ICU. My head had been shaved in strips, preserving some hair that could be combed over my bald patches. Twenty-seven staples dotted my skull. Stitches, too. Two metal plates were secured in the back of my head, while two screws held my skull together. My face was bruised and swollen. IVs were attached to both arms.

As I began to regain consciousness in the ICU, I was vaguely aware of people talking around me. I faded in and out of foggy slumber.

The next day, a nurse pried my eye open, shining a bright light into my pupil.

"Do you know where you are?" she asked.

I nodded, knowing I was at the hospital in Memphis.

She asked, "What's your name?"

"Ti-nee," I answered. The words coming out of my mouth sounded more garbled than they did in my head.

"Do you know why you're here, Tiffany?" she inquired.

I nodded again.

"Why are you here?" she asked.

"Bain surgy."

Bain surgy? Why couldn't I speak? My lips seemed to wrestle against one another, unable to form clear sounds.

When the nurse paused to check other vital functions, I glanced over at my mom, sitting next to my bed beside my dad.

"Hi, honey," she cooed. "How are you?"

Groggy and disoriented, I struggled to stay conscious. I was vaguely aware of the nurse, poking and prodding, and others moving about the room.

Monitors beeped. Liquids sloshed. I smelled dried blood.

"You did great, Tiffany," my mom assured me. "And the doctor thinks he got it all. You're such a trooper, honey."

THE DEVIL'S SCHEMES

The devil hasn't given up on destroying God's plans for our generation. He's still at work to steal, kill, and destroy. You may be facing an illness, injury, or disability that threatens to undo you. Or the deceiver may be at work in your mind, hissing guilt and lies and shame, making you doubt God's gracious gift of salvation and sanctification. Or maybe you're facing financial challenges. The devil may tempt you with relationships that compromise your deep beliefs. The enemy is busily about the business of sin and death.

While God's goal is life, the enemy's goal for our generation is death. A majority of us struggle with self-image, self-absorption, and self-worth. We battle depression, shame, and life-stealing thoughts. We also fall into the trap of lust and immoral living. If you're among the majority of women who struggle with one of these issues, and you have a relationship with Christ, I suspect that you desire to live the blessed plan God has for your life but haven't stopped to think about the severity of these dark schemes of Satan.

Because your mind is the gateway to your heart, Satan attempts to thwart God's plan for your life by attacking you with lies that corrupt God's Word and His promises. Sinking tentacles of despair into your mind, Satan steals away any hope of fully living God's plan with joy and freedom. Plaguing you with self-image issues, relational stresses, addictions, and insecurity, he distracts you from the fulfilled life that you and I were called to live.

Though I don't want to glorify Satan, I do want to expose the reality the enemy's schemes attempt to mask: God designed you and me to live meaningful lives of purpose, free from the darkness of the world. To take hold of the abundant plan God has for us, we need to get serious about rooting out all that's deadly from our minds. We can do so with confidence, knowing we are not alone in the battle; God is a mighty warrior who wages war for us. We're called to join in the fight by girding ourselves with prayer and fasting and nourishing ourselves with God's Word. With God's power, we can wriggle free from the devil's grip and remove all that's toxic from our lives.

The boyfriend who disrespects you and makes you feel inadequate is toxic.

Scrolling through images on social media that cause you to compare yourself to others is toxic.

Dwelling on the lie that your identity is rooted in your past is toxic.

Comparing the call on your life to the call of God on another woman's life is toxic.

Believing the lie that someone spoke to you is toxic.

The same way my surgeon loosened the devil's grip on my brain, by carefully removing each wily finger of the tumor, you can eliminate what's choking the life out of you—first, by identifying the darkness in your life, and second, by shining God's light into that darkness with the help of Jesus and other believers.

Because God's dream for this world is being accomplished through the followers of Jesus, those of us who take God at His word by aligning our minds with truth and making ourselves available to carry out His plan are dangerous to the forces of darkness.

If you want to live a life that matters, if you long to partner with God to accomplish the unimaginable, you can expect resistance. But I can assure you that the battle has already been won. It's time for you to walk in freedom.

UNAWARE

When I woke up from my fourth surgery, I had no idea what I was facing. Though the medical team and my parents were beginning to suspect what might lie ahead for me, I was completely oblivious. I understood that surgery takes a toll on the whole body, and I believed I'd simply need to work at regaining strength and function.

I didn't realize the enemy had hit me where it would hurt the most.

CHAPTER 4

FIGHTING MY WAY BACK

Our focus on the body isn't God's priority.

Groggy from medication, drifting in and out of consciousness, I woke up in a recovery room. Swollen and bruised, stitched and stapled, I was still hooked up to IVs and monitors and tubes.

"Hi, honey," my mom whispered. "How are you feeling?"

" 'Kay," I spit out, not sounding quite like myself.

My dad queried, "Do you have any pain?"

"Nah bah," I heard myself say. *Not bad.*

I assumed my slurred speech was from the medications I'd been given.

Realizing they were drilling me with questions, my mom switched gears. "Gentry and Bradley say hi."

As we spoke, I felt my parents looking at me. Not at my eyes, but at my face. I knew from other surgeries that the swelling and bruising and dried blood looked pretty gross.

A nurse came into my room, introduced herself, and began asking me questions.

"Tiffany, can you move your right leg for me?" she asked, pointing at my right leg.

I lifted my right leg. Farthest from my head and face, it was the body part that hurt the least!

"Great, and can you lift your left leg?"

I tried, but my leg didn't cooperate. Was it tangled up under the sheets?

"Tiffany, can you lift your right arm?" the nurse asked, pointing at my right arm.

I lifted my arm dutifully. My mom smiled.

"And can you lift your left arm?"

My left arm didn't move. I thought it must be pinned down with tubes or sheets. I tried to lift it but couldn't. It wouldn't budge.

Though my immobility was frustrating, I didn't fully understand what had happened. I assumed that when the swelling went down, the weakness would dissipate and my motor skills would return.

TEST RUN

For the first thirty-six hours, I had a catheter and was fed intravenously. But the second day after my surgery, I wanted to use the restroom situated just three feet from my bed.

Anticipating weakness, a nurse suggested that she support me on one side and my mom and dad support me on the other. They helped me sit up and scoot to the edge of the bed. Stepping carefully toward the floor, I planted my right foot, then my left. As I stood to bear weight, though, I collapsed.

I fell into my dad, who caught me.

"Whoa, got ya!" he said as he helped me stand upright again.

As I felt my legs beneath me, I realized my affliction wasn't "weakness." My left side was entirely immobilized. Slowly moving toward the bathroom, I was keenly aware that it was the strength of my parents and the nurse that was getting me there.

After helping me get to the restroom, the nurse and

my dad gave my mom and me some privacy. Because I had no balance, my mom supported me. I sensed that my mom was nervous.

A few minutes later, when I was finished, the nurse returned to help me stand. The small bathroom was a tight squeeze for the three of us, but they carefully helped me pivot to stand in front of the sink.

I hadn't looked in a mirror since before the surgery, and I was shocked by what I saw.

Because I'd had brain surgery before, I'd expected the swelling and bruising. I'd even reconciled myself to the horrible bald strips where my hair had been shaved. But I was not prepared for what I saw in the mirror.

Under the bandages stretching across my forehead, I could see that the left and right sides of my face didn't match. Despite the swollenness, I recognized the girl on the right. My right eye and right side of my mouth looked like me.

The left side of my face, however, was unrecognizable. My eye and cheek and mouth drooped lifelessly. It looked like the face of someone I'd feel pity for. Eyes forward, I lifted my eyebrows, but only one moved. Though the last thing I felt like doing was smiling, I willed a small smile. The right corner of my mouth responded, lifting my cheek with it, but the left side remained lifeless.

During the time I'd spent in bed since the surgery, I was aware that my speaking had been compromised. I heard my slurred speech. But staring at the twisted face looking back at me in the mirror, I began to realize that the paralysis of my face and the uselessness of my entire left side might not be as temporary as I imagined.

Supporting my weight, the nurse turned on the

water; then, picking up my left arm for me, she and my mom applied soap to my hands. Gently rubbing them together, they rinsed them under warm water.

I could see a tear running down my mom's cheek.

Catching my glance, she assured me, "Tiff, everything's going to work together for good. God has something wonderful ahead of you. He'll heal your face. It'll be fine."

Though she was being brave for me, I recognized confidence mingling with a hint of caution in her voice.

As the nurse dried my hands with a paper towel as if I were a toddler, I couldn't take my eyes off the mirror.

Because of all the metal plates and screws holding my skull together, my body wouldn't tolerate the pressure on an airplane. So five days after surgery I was wheeled out to our car that my dad had driven back to Memphis. When a nurse and my dad carefully lifted me from the wheelchair into the backseat of our car, I realized how helpless I was outside of the hospital.

Six hours after we left Memphis, we were pulling into the driveway of our home.

My dad helped me to our guest bedroom on the first floor. But with the left side of my body being useless, it was closer to carrying. When he gently laid me down in the bed, it had never felt better.

Though I wasn't able to walk to either the mirror over the dresser or the one in the bathroom, I'd caught glimpses of my reflection on the car ride home. I had no desire to look again. Maybe it would be better for me, mentally, if I didn't know what I looked like.

Disabled, deformed, distraught, I felt the dreams I'd had for my life being shattered.

REHAB

We'd arrived home on Sunday, December 23. The next morning I was in therapy. I was still so weak from surgery that it was hard to sit up in my wheelchair. My left leg was weak, but with the slightest bit of strength left. My arm was stubborn, completely unresponsive. I simply could not will it to move. I had no movement in my hand.

Before we left St. Jude's, we were warned that what function I didn't recover in six weeks, I probably wouldn't recover at all. This was our cue to get involved in rehab as soon as possible. It worked. I stayed out of school for six weeks in order to invest every ounce of energy into physical therapy.

I was determined to make my six weeks count.

Monday through Friday I spent four to five hours in therapy. Much of the session was spent training my leg. One of the techniques to retrain my arm was to have a towel under both hands, on a table surface, that I'd wipe like I was cleaning a table. With both arms moving in mirror fashion, the left side of the brain controlling my strong right side and the right side of the brain controlling my resistant left side, the hope was that both sides would move in sync.

I've never worked as hard as I did during those six weeks.

When I returned home each afternoon, I was completely exhausted—mentally and physically. When my limbs weren't being manipulated by a therapist. . .when a parent wasn't pushing my wheelchair. . .when I was alone in my room. . .my lack of ability was undeniable.

I couldn't sit up in bed independently, let alone walk

to the bathroom. Day and night I used my cell to call my mom to come help me.

Bathing was most humiliating. After helping me undress, my mom would wrap me in a towel to preserve the shred of dignity I had left. She would support my left side while I used the strength on my right side to get into the tub. Using only my right arm to support myself, she'd help lower me into the tub. I'd do as much as I could with my right arm, but I needed her to wash, rinse, and then dry my hair.

I hated my dependence. I hated feeling like an infant.

I was completely incapable.

Day after day, week after week, it was terribly hard for me to notice any progress. From my perspective *everything*—my face, my hair, my body's lack of function-ality—was all *worse* than it had been before the surgery. The surgery didn't even stop my seizures, which wasn't uncommon. The hope was that when my brain was com-pletely healed, the seizures would disappear.

Life "pre-surgery" could no longer be the measuring stick for my progress. We were forced to measure prog-ress from the moment of my stroke, when my blood vessel was nicked in surgery. And though my droopy left eye struggled to perceive any improvement, others who'd seen me in the days after surgery were able to see small increments of progress.

Although my parents and Gentry and Bradley under-stood, at some level, what a horrifying experience it was to have suffered a stroke that paralyzed my body, I tried to stay strong. Though I was crushed, I attempted to hide the extent of my devastation from just about everyone.

The only one who felt the full extent of my sadness was God. I felt like everything had been stripped from me. I lay awake in bed for hours each night, crying out to God. I'd never felt more broken.

RETURN TO SCHOOL

After my first six weeks of full-time therapy ended, I returned to school, half days at first, after the first week of February.

The last time many schoolmates had seen me was at homecoming, when Gentry and I were both on the homecoming court. Though my friends had been anticipating my return to school, a casual observer or a substitute teacher could not have identified me as the same girl.

Everything about "day one" was rough. Because I'd gone to therapy for the first half of the day, I was wiped out. Too weak to walk the length of Jenks High's campus, I returned in a wheelchair. As a nurse pushed me through the front entrance of the school, while most of the students were in class or at lunch, I was excited to be back but also embarrassed to be returning so broken. The secretary who helped me sign in at the main office was the first one to look at me with the pitiful glance that would become all too familiar. Even those students who smiled and said hello, attempting to act normal, weren't good enough actors to pull it off. I saw that they were trying to act normal in a situation that was far from it. In their faces I saw the pity I despised.

Gentry pushed me between classes and helped me as I struggled to wedge myself, in the wheelchair, under each desk. Between classes she assisted me in the restroom. Gentry had helped me fix my hair to hide my scar and cover the patches of six-week stubble that were growing back in, but it was still pretty rough. My arm was bound by a sling to protect my shoulder. While the bruising and swelling had gone down, my face bore every sign of my stroke. As desperately as I wanted to be like every other student, I still could not will the left side of my face to respond to my brain's cues.

It took every ounce of courage I had to swallow my pride and show up every day.

I was determined to get out of that wheelchair. And two weeks after I returned, I was able to limp between classes. Between each class, a friend would carry my books as I put all of my energy into dragging my body to my next class. Step, drag. Step, drag. Step, drag. After each strong step with my right leg, I'd lift my left leg at the hip, dragging it forward.

MY FACE

What bothered me most was my face.

The left side of my face, refusing to obey the simplest commands my brain sent its way, drooped stubbornly. My lid slumped lifelessly. My cheek and half of my mouth sagged. The half of my face that was able to smile looked like a sixteen-year-old; the sagging side looked like someone decades older who lacked all muscle control.

At sixteen, I felt horrified by my twisted features. If I'd had the choice, I would have chosen permanent paralysis in a wheelchair over the lifeless face I was forced to wear.

I'd work on it during my therapy sessions, and when I came home at night I'd sit in front of my bedside mirror for hours repeating the drills I'd learned during the day.

I'd use my hand to hold up the limp side of my mouth while smiling, to remind my muscles how they were supposed to behave. I'd attempt to contort my face into the dramatic expressions of a stage actress—in horror, surprise, anger, or joy—to gain some recognizable expression. When I could elicit no movement from the left side, I'd break down crying.

And I prayed.

I prayed for my face, giving God very clear instructions. "If You heal my face, I'll do these things for You. . . ." I'd list a few sacrificial acts, but in the event I'd missed any biggies that really mattered to God, I'd always add, "I'll do *anything* You tell me to do if You just do this one thing for me." The alternate rhythm of working on my exercises and praying for God to intervene became my nightly routine. It began with a strong prayer pleading for healing then continued with the mirror exercises that seemed to produce little change. Day after day, I limped along, feeling distorted. Like I'd lost my value.

BODIES AND SOULS

I didn't consider myself particularly shallow or superficial. I was, in fact, like just about every girl I knew. Shaped by a culture that values physical appearance over true beauty, I wanted to be perceived as attractive by others. Persuaded by magazines and billboards, television shows and other girls at school, I'd bought the lie that I was valued for my appearance.

Maybe you've been persuaded to believe the lie that you are more valuable when you can meet culture's criteria for physical attractiveness and are less valuable when you don't. When we can't scroll through our phones without seeing flawless, filtered beauty, it's easy for the world's definition of what's attractive—long flowing hair, a perfectly contoured face, a toned physique—to define us.

Yet, while the world is focused on what people look like on the outside, God is concerned about beauty on the inside. We cultivate true beauty when we invest in who God made us to be.

Despite my pleading prayers, my face wasn't healed overnight. But God was doing a much deeper healing in my heart. As my weak body slowly started to improve, my perspective began to shift. While I was focused on fine-tuning the paralyzed muscles in my face, the Lord was focused on fine-tuning the muscles of my heart. I discovered that God was less concerned with eliminating my insecurities and more concerned with who I was becoming in the midst of them. Intent on strengthening my faith, developing my character, and shifting my focus away from worldly standards, God was preparing me to trade in the physical appearance I valued for a "true beauty" that does not fade (1 Peter 3:3–4).

The reality is that we live in a world consumed with our bodies, yet we serve a Father who's consumed with our souls. As we obsess over things that will one day perish, God pays attention only to what's eternal. God is inviting women in our generation to surrender their desire for a beautiful outward appearance for an inward beauty found only in Christ.

If your perspective on beauty has been focused more on physical appearance than on who you are becoming, now is the time to examine your heart. Because God is more concerned with building our faith than with improving our situations, He wants to bring truth, healing, and restoration to the deep insecurities we bear by revealing to us beauty as He meant it to be.

The most beautiful people I've ever met weren't ladies with perfect figures and features. They were women who'd overcome adversity, walked with steadfast faith, and lived differently than the women around them. It was impossible not to take notice of them!

It would be a few more years before God truly gave me new vision and reordered my priorities. Until then, I'd pour everything I had into being just like every other girl.

Or at least like the girl I once was.

FRIEND TIME

Two months after I came home from St. Jude's, my dad dropped me off at the mall so I could pick up a tie and picture frame I'd been planning to get him for his birthday. A semester earlier I would have been driving myself in my own car, but the seizure, operation, and stroke had reduced me to the dependency of a child.

Though I was no longer using a wheelchair, I was still self-conscious about my appearance. The hair that had been shaved was growing in, like a crew cut, alongside my longer hair. My left arm was in a sling, as if I was a typical girl who'd broken it while cheerleading. Without the sling, it hung lifeless. My right side remained strong, but it takes two good sides to walk! So my left leg just dragged along after the right one.

After picking up my dad's present, I limped toward the mall entrance where his car was idling. It was 3:57.

"Thanks, Dad," I greeted him as I fell into the passenger seat.

"Hi, babe. Everything go okay?" he asked.

Before I could answer, I sensed my body about to

betray me. I felt tingling in my hand that climbed up my arm and rippled through my whole body. Unable to even warn my dad, I just leaned over and succumbed to the shaking and jerking that I couldn't control. My dad flipped off the engine while he supported my head.

"I got you, sweetheart," he said. "I'm getting help right now."

Cradling my head with his left arm and hand, he used his right hand to call 911.

I heard him telling the operator, "My daughter is having a seizure and we need help immediately. Woodlands Mall, outside of the food court. . ."

Then my world went black.

I regained consciousness about five minutes later. My dad, cradling me in his strong arms, was praying. I heard the sounds of distant sirens getting closer. When the paramedics arrived, the seizure had passed and I was fully conscious. My father explained my history as they examined me. Because I hadn't suffered injury, they allowed me to go home with my dad.

While it might seem like it would be hard for me to find things for which to be grateful, that day was different. I was grateful I hadn't been at school.

A shy girl, I didn't want to receive any extra attention. My saggy face and limp walk were bad enough, but my biggest fear was that I'd have a major seizure at school. Daily I was afraid, while sitting in class, that I'd begin to seize and fall from my chair to the floor. With a complete loss of control, I knew I could make strange sounds like a wild animal and had heard of others who were epileptic who had wet themselves. Nothing would have been more humiliating. If it happened in my dad's car, it could happen at school.

Every moment I was in public, every moment I was at school, I lived with the knowledge that at any moment, without warning, I could have a seizure.

RETURN TO ST. JUDE'S

Seizures hadn't been unexpected post-surgery. But because I'd suffered one after the swelling had gone down in my brain, radiation was prescribed to ensure there wasn't any tumor left in my brain.

The second week of March, just eleven weeks after I'd returned home, I moved to Memphis to begin six weeks of radiation treatments. I stayed at the Ronald McDonald House, and family members—my mom, dad, sister, brother, grandparents—would join me different weeks for support, encouragement, and transportation.

A combination mask and helmet was custom-sculpted so my head could be screwed to a table during treatments. This kept my skull perfectly still, ensuring that the laser could target and reach the correct area of the brain.

I was one of the first patients to be treated with a new type of radiation that directly radiated the affected area of the brain instead of the entire brain. All of my efforts to save my hair went out the window during the first week of treatments, when chunks of my hair started coming out by the handful. Rather than shaving off what was left, I kept it all different lengths. Constant nausea and weakness meant that doing physical therapy and staying on top of my schoolwork became extra difficult.

But nothing was going to keep me from fighting my way back to "normal."

Chapter 5

WHAT A GIRL WANTS

God's dream is different than our plans.

From the age of ten I'd been poked and prodded, medicated and operated on, treated and released. Everyone in my community knew I was "that girl." And as I anticipated beginning my freshman year at Oklahoma State University, all I wanted was to be normal.

No baldness.

No wheelchair.

No limp.

No disfigurement.

Just a normal girl.

I knew what I wanted out of life, and I felt competent enough to get it.

Had I closed my eyes and pictured my future, it would have looked like the dreams of a lot of girls I knew: I'd be dating a cute, godly guy, and we would fall in love. A few years after our stunning wedding, we'd start a family. He'd have a great job he was passionate about, and I'd be a stay-at-home mom, raising our children. Because that's a luxury, I'd have my own event-planning business on the side. We'd enjoy a comfortable income and live in a picturesque home with a pool on a secluded property with some land outside of Tulsa.

That was the dream in my heart as I started college. It was ambitious. . .

But if I had all that, I'd be set.

OSU

Caffeine and sleeplessness—staples of normal college life—were two triggers for seizures. And though I'd been seizure-free for a year and a half, my parents didn't want to risk my health to dorm life. So they bought a house in Stillwater where I lived with my sister, Gentry, and her sorority sister.

Nothing was more normal at OSU than rushing a sorority.

In the fall I rushed Chi Omega. Though movies about Greek life can make rush look pretty grueling, my health didn't limit me. If you enjoy standing in the Oklahoma heat for hours and having the same conversation thirty times in a row, then rush is a great experience. Though I still struggled to walk long distances and had some facial paralysis on my left side, most students didn't notice. And if they did, they at least didn't give me the looks of pity I'd grown to disdain in high school.

The girls in my pledge class of 2007 soon became my closest friends. Stephanie and I were both "legacies," which meant we had older sisters in Chi Omega. We actually met our junior year of high school on legacy night and became good friends. I met Lauren in high school, too, when she'd come to a Jenks football game with a friend I knew.

Stephanie and I ran into Lauren at an OSU event the spring before rushing. At that time her plans had been to go to Africa as a missionary for a year before going to Oral Roberts University to prepare for a career in ministry. Unable to fathom why anyone would want to turn down sorority life to move to Africa, Steph and I eventually talked her into OSU and rushing with us.

My sorority sisters were all so different. Jackie was a high school pom captain. Stephanie was a Houston volleyball player. Racheal was the small-town, country girl. Lauren was the homeschooled creative. Kelly, the former color guard captain. And the list went on. There were girls who lived on farms and girls from prestigious private schools, girls who wanted to be doctors and girls who wanted to meet their husbands.

Then there was me.

Every girl had her unique thing. Mine just happened to be "former cancer patient."

Despite our interest in monograms, Starbucks, and oversized T-shirts, most of us had little in common. Yet suddenly we were thrown into the Chi Omega sorority world together, which meant study hours, costume date parties, football games, intramural sports, and Coke dates. I was learning how to dress for game day, shoot water balloons off frat house rooftops, persuasively convince teachers I deserved a higher grade, and fit countless Vera Bradley duffel bags into the back of an SUV for a sixteen-hour road trip to Destin, Florida, for spring break.

My friends were solid, and my life was shaping up according to my plan.

Life was *so* normal.

SUMMER SNOW

Since I was on track to own an event-planning business, I chose to major in hotel and restaurant administration. During my freshman year, when a fraternity friend told me that he'd owned three snow cone stands back in the small town where he lived, and I realized how young he was, a spark ignited inside me. When Gentry and I were little, we would color pictures in our Lisa Frank coloring book, and instead of giving them to our parents, like most children, we would stage a store in our playroom and make our mom and dad *buy* them from us! I've always had an entrepreneurial spirit. If my friend had run a business, I didn't see why I couldn't, too.

The summer after freshman year I bought a trailer that we hauled to a Blockbuster parking lot, where it lived for the summer months—rent-free! My first legit business venture was called Summer Snow. I hired part-time employees to man the trailer while I focused on managing, supplying, and promoting the business. My very first employee was my younger brother, Bradley, who was thirteen at the time.

I lived at home that summer, mixing huge tubs of sugar water in my parents' kitchen. Bradley and I would boil water in five-gallon pots and mix in fifty pounds of sugar. When it was thoroughly mixed, I'd add the flavor concentrate: grape, cherry, strawberry, and more. Then I'd pour the syrup mixture into quart bottles we'd use in the trailer to flavor the shaved ice. My poor mom's nice kitchen became a sticky mess just about every day.

Oklahoma summers are hot, and our customers loved summer snow.

I loved building a business from the ground up. It wouldn't be my last.

UP 'TIL DAWN

When I was still in high school, Gentry had told me that the Sigma Nu fraternity at OSU hosted an annual fund-raiser for St. Jude's called Up 'til Dawn. Though the all-night sleepless event—from 6:00 p.m. Friday to 6:00 a.m. Saturday—wasn't optimal for patients or recent survivors, it was a lot of fun for the OSU students who participated! Students raised money before the event and then stayed up for an all-night party. There was a fun kickoff event with games and food. Throughout the event there were videos, games, and prizes. Educational moments featured patients who shared their stories.

Early in my sophomore year, St. Jude's called and asked me if I'd like to be one of the speakers at Up 'til Dawn. The short answer was no. For a host of reasons, I really didn't want to be one of the speakers. For starters, I was terrified of public speaking. In high school I'd taken a public speaking class and hated it. Second, one of the side effects of my surgery was that I had lost my short-term memory. I could prepare all day for a two-minute speech and still not remember it. Third, I had worked really hard in college to be super normal. Very few people on campus knew my story, and I hardly wanted to stand on a podium and announce it into a microphone!

In the end, I came to my senses. My gratitude to St. Jude's trumped both my fear of public speaking and even my being outed as the "sick girl." After all, without St. Jude's, I knew I wouldn't even be alive. Speaking at the event was the least I could do for the hospital.

The event took place in the student union auditorium. It was a large open room filled with round tables, like a banquet hall. Projectors flooded the walls with stories of children whose lives had been rescued at St. Jude's. Most of the students in the room wore the white "Up 'til Dawn" event T-shirt with turquoise print.

As a video about St. Jude's concluded, an emcee introduced me.

I was sitting at one of the tables with Gentry. As the emcee spoke, I began to feel nauseated. Not as bad as from radiation, but not great either. My heart raced, and my hands felt shaky.

". . .OSU sophomore, Tiffany Smiling!"

As the emcee concluded his intro, I drew a deep breath and stood to walk up to the platform. I was painfully aware of hundreds of eyes on me.

My cover as "normal" had been blown.

I was wearing jeans and a flowery coral top. I swept my hair out of my face and stepped up to the microphone, clutching my notes.

"Hi," I began. "I'm Tiffany. When I was ten years old, I started having seizures. My family and I went from doctor to doctor, seeking answers, but were turned down at hospital after hospital. Other doctors were afraid to operate, and one gave me just three months to live."

Though I still felt the audience's gaze, I was encouraged by their attentiveness. I glanced over at my girlfriends in the audience and was encouraged by the support I saw in their eyes.

I continued, "When we visited St. Jude's, Dr. Sanford agreed to operate. We knew it was a risky operation, but St. Jude's gave us hope."

I described having three surgeries and radiation at St. Jude's, as well as how amazing they were to accommodate and serve us. At the end of my speech, I confirmed what students were hearing throughout the evening: "St. Jude's is changing childhood cancer."

Honestly, although I was a bit uncomfortable talking about myself, I loved singing the praises of St. Jude's. As I struggled to place the microphone back in its stand, I noticed my hands were still jittery. But as the audience erupted in applause, the rest of me felt awash with relief. When I reached my seat, Gentry, grinning from ear to ear, embraced me in a huge hug.

My story was out, and there was no putting it back in the box.

Maybe because I'd had the opportunity to get established my freshman year, to be known as a regular girl, sharing my story didn't feel as raw as I feared it might. My sorority sisters, some who'd had no idea I'd battled cancer, were extremely supportive of me. And after that evening, a number of curious guy friends around campus let me know that they'd been at the event and asked me more about my story.

That felt all right.

One of the young men in the room that night was a guy I'd started dating at the beginning of the school year, whom I'll call Dave. We'd met freshman year at a Chi Omega party and had hit it off right away. He was a Christian, and we were part of the same large friend group.

ORANGE LEAF

Dave and I dated throughout our sophomore year and were getting closer when we began our junior year. We found time in our full schedules to see each other.

My junior year also held another sweetness in store.

If I'd dipped my toe into the entrepreneurial world with Summer Snow, my junior year of college I would get my whole foot wet.

It was no secret at Chi Omega that I loved ice cream. Truly, I would eat it every day. So when my friend Jackie was driving to her hometown of Edmond for a hair appointment, she invited me to come with her and check out a little frozen yogurt joint there, called Orange Leaf.

Let me just say, I was up for the adventure.

We walked into Orange Leaf, and I loved what I saw. Two walls were lined with self-serve style ice cream pumps, with more flavors than I could dream of: peanut butter, fudge brownie, birthday cake, you name it! And there was also a toppings bar—with more treats than a candy store—featuring all kinds of chocolates, cereals, sprinkles, gummies, and more. It was the first time I'd ever seen a self-serve frozen yogurt store, and I loved it! It was fun. It was family friendly. And my hometown of Tulsa didn't have anything like it.

With this idea bubbling inside me, I returned home and began praying about the potential. I knew that if I waited eighteen months until graduation, it would be too late. Someone would have gotten the jump on us. Needing advice, I pitched the plan to my dad who, in addition to being an attorney, was a businessman. He told me to go for it and get a loan! As I researched what it took to establish an Orange Leaf franchise, he coached me through the process and an Oklahoma bank gave me a loan.

I was excited about this journey ahead but wanted to seek God's wisdom before signing the papers. I had the loan, I had the franchise agreement—all I needed was the Lord's consent that this was the plan He had for me. I asked God to show me a sign of guidance for this decision. Guess what I asked Him for. Yep, an *orange leaf*. (When I pray embarrassing prayers like this, I don't tell a soul.)

As I gazed out my window the next few days, I

realized how humorous my prayer must have sounded in God's ear. It was mid-January in Oklahoma, and there wasn't any color of leaf in sight! But I'd peek out my window every morning when I woke up, just in case the Lord wanted to surprise me.

A week later, at the end of my human resources class, I received a text from Steph, asking me to come over and help her make costumes for a Chi Omega date party we were pumped up for. As I walked toward the parking lot, the earth was blanketed in fresh white snow. But as I got closer to my car, I was shocked and confused by what I saw. Though the trees were bare, without a single leaf in sight for miles, a carpet of orange leaves covered the ground around my car.

Really, God?

This was the first time I recognized God speaking to me.

Once I'd received the beautiful direction from God, I was all in.

"I will put one in Tulsa," I vowed, "before anyone else does."

Two days after I spotted the orange leaves around my car, I signed the papers to open my own Orange Leaf franchise.

If I had paused to measure the progress I was making toward my dreams—earning my degree, dating a great guy, launching my business—I would have found I was right on track to be living the dream after graduation.

A BEGINNING AND AN ENDING

Throughout my junior year I loved the challenge of launching my store. From finding the perfect location to supervising the building process, the adventure was full of excitement.

But as the business began to take shape, my relationship with Dave started to disintegrate. Though we both still cared for each other, I gradually discovered that Dave was not the guy he presented himself to be. He was making choices that hurt him and hurt me. Though I asked him, with love, to change, he was unwilling or unable to do it.

That disappointment wasn't at all what I'd expected from a relationship. I'd grown up in a home with a godly dad and a godly brother. I had no other expectation, from childhood, than that I'd meet a godly man who loved the Lord and respected women. But that wasn't my experience with Dave. While he certainly believed in God, his sin triggered some of the deep insecurities God was still healing in me.

Would he have been satisfied with me if I hadn't been paralyzed?

Would he have made different choices if I'd looked a different way?

And there was the hurt. I felt I had a lot to offer. I believed that if he cared enough for me, he would change. He'd make better choices. Propelled by his love for me and for the Lord, he'd do whatever it took to make the right choices. But he didn't. And the voice of the deceiver took advantage of that fact to shout that I wasn't good enough.

Around Thanksgiving of my junior year, I ended our relationship.

Though common sense might suggest that it's easier to be the "dumper" than the "dumpee," I can tell you that's not true at all. I hadn't wanted our relationship to end the way it did. Even though I'd ended our relationship, I was very hurt in the aftermath.

I felt like I hadn't been enough to fight for.

A DREAM REALIZED, A DREAM DEFERRED

Remember that dream of mine—with the husband, kids, and white picket fence?

I'd always known that I wanted to be a professional and also stay at home with my kids. I knew I could get ahead of the game by developing a profitable business on the front end that would provide the income that would make my dream possible. When I opened the first self-serve frozen dessert franchise in Tulsa, I was making progress toward realizing that dream.

But parts of that dream were outside my control. Meeting the husband God had for me was one of those pieces.

This would actually be the piece that would begin to loosen my grip on all the other pieces.

If the dream you've had for your life hasn't yet panned out, it's worth pausing to compare your dream to God's dream for you. Just as I was, a lot of young women are after a comfortable life. We may paint it with other strokes, but if we're completely honest, we're seeking our own happiness and comfort. To be fair, it's how most of us have been raised. Whether we were captivated by stories of fairy-tale princesses or another charming vision of love, comfort, and security, it's in our nature to pursue pleasure over pain, satisfaction over want, love over loneliness. It's natural.

But God was about to teach me that the crumbling of my dream could make room for His plan for me and for the greater needs of the world. If only I'd been able to see through the blinding pain, I might have recognized that my dream wasn't quite big enough.

God's dream isn't the same as the American dream. In fact, the American dream—the one I'd imagined—has been designed more by picture-perfect Pinterest feeds than by the One who is the author of your story and mine. Movies will occasionally present a heroine who makes sacrifices in order to access better options for her life. But more often than not the story ends in comfortable, domestic wedded bliss.

Believe me, I'm not knocking wedded bliss!

But I want you to hear that you have been created to accomplish mighty things for the Lord beyond your current circumstances.

And if, like me, you discover the dream you had for your life has been sidetracked—because you haven't met that guy, or because you haven't yet discovered and embraced God's purpose for your life—this moment, pause and ask for God's wisdom.

Ask Him to show you His vision for the areas in your life that aren't yet aligned with His good plan for you.

Chapter 6

EIGHTEEN WEDDINGS AND ONE NEW LOVE

Comparing yourself and your story to others is deadly.

I glanced down at my phone and recognized the number. It was one of my employees at the store.

I slipped out from behind my desk in econ class, as if I were leaving to use the restroom, walked down the hallway a bit, and dialed her back.

"Hey, what's up?" I asked. "Mmm-hmm. . . Okay. . . Yeah, the spoons are on the second shelf in the supply closet. See 'em? Big cube box? . . . Great. . . Okay, bye."

I'd never planned to be a full-time student running a business, but during my final semester of college, that's exactly what I was. Because of the online coursework I'd done, I was able to graduate from college in seven semesters. So my final semester was the fall after I'd opened Orange Leaf, the summer before my senior year. That meant that employees—one full-time and five part-time— would call with questions, large and small, more often than my professors knew and more often than I would have preferred. I managed what I could by e-mail, text, and phone, and I traveled the ninety minutes to the shop in Tulsa about once a week.

Dave and I had broken up the previous fall, just as I was preparing to begin construction on the store. That meant that even though my heart was stinging, my life had been so full that I'd pushed through the pain instead of making the space I needed to fully heal. For the first six months the store was open, I was pretty much in constant motion, without time or space to move past the hurts that surfaced after my breakup with Dave.

After the fall semester, I continued to live in Stillwater near my friends. I'd made a deal with my parents that if I graduated in seven semesters, I could live in the Stillwater house through graduation in May. I could run the store from there and still not miss out on my last spring break, last round of date parties, and the memories I was making with my girlfriends.

Did I mention that most of them were *engaged*?

The wedding invitations started trickling in at the end of February. They continued to be delivered over the course of several months. That semester when I was no longer a student, I finally did have time to grieve my breakup with Dave. Receiving those beautiful wedding invitations—to ceremonies scheduled between our May graduation and Thanksgiving—only made the grieving process more difficult.

By the time all was said and done, eighteen wedding invitations had been delivered to my mailbox. And I'd been invited to be a bridesmaid in six of them.

When we graduated in May, my friends and I were sad in the sense that we all were moving away from our glorious days in Stillwater. But instead of saying goodbye, we were able to say, "See you next weekend." And we'd say the same thing the next weekend, and the one after that!

If you're like a lot of single girls I know, in their twenties and thirties, you've attended your fair share of weddings. Beyond the wedding itself, you attended the shower, played the shower games, and traveled out of town for the bachelorette party. If the wedding was out of town, you saved up the money and bought the plane ticket and the hotel room. If you were invited to join the wedding party, you also purchased a bridesmaid dress and hosted the wedding festivities on behalf of your beloved girl. And if you were smart, you stocked up and filled your closet with some thoughtful and useful wedding gifts, like Martha Stewart cookbooks and MacKenzie-Childs dishes.

Though I could rejoice with my friends, I also began asking God some hard questions, trying to make sense of how my life was unfolding.

Why, God?

Why did Dave hurt me, after I'd shared the hardest parts of my story with him?

Why has my whole path been so different from the paths of those around me?

Ever since my stroke, I'd wrestled with God. I wanted to know why everyone else was able to live their life any way they chose, and everything seemed to fall into place, but I'd been saddled with cancer, seizures, radiation, a stroke, and rehab. And now finding a godly man with whom to spend the rest of my life was proving to be more difficult as well.

My prayer time was the safe space where I could lay my heart bare before the Lord. A logical thinker, searching for meaning, I wrestled to make sense of everything that had happened to me. God listened patiently, as He does to every cry of our hearts.

But what I didn't realize at the time is how dangerous it is to compare our stories to others'. That kind of comparison assumes that we are *due* happiness, that we are entitled to the blessing of "God's plan," even if we didn't seek Him in all the pursuits that have left us empty and alone. It assumes our path should look like the paths others have walked or are walking.

This generation has been called the OCD (obsessive comparison disorder) generation. Whether we're glued to social media on our phones throughout the day, or whether we peek during downtime at work or at school, we're constantly bombarded with filtered images of others' lives. Even when the images aren't technically touched up, they've still been selected as the best of the batch! What we don't see on social media are the days and nights when a friend is crushed by depression. We don't see the emotional pain of rejection. We don't know about her recovery from the physical and emotional pain of abuse. Nor are we privy to other kinds of physical suffering. We never get a glimpse of a broken heart. All we see are the highlight reels, grinning selfies with polished hair and makeup, that distort what lives are really like. We naturally compare our own lives—the hurts, the bumps, the disappointments, the scars—and find them lacking.

We want her blessings without her battles. Her accomplishments without her agony. Her prosperity without her pain. Her luxuries without her longings.

And the spiritual danger in comparing our stories to others'—hoping our lives look more like their highs—is that God's plan for their lives *should* look different from His plan for our own. The risk of comparison is that we miss out on the specific, strategic, handcrafted story God is writing through each of our lives.

Still, I found myself tangled up in the deadly trap of comparison. *She* was able to find a great guy to marry. *Her* face is perfectly symmetrical. *She* doesn't have a limp. Though I wanted to believe my differences were imperceptible to others, when I'd be out in public, people would ask, "What's wrong with your foot?" or "Did you break your leg?"

As I celebrated the season of attending so many friends' weddings, I asked God why their lives had unfolded so neatly and mine had not. But as I offered that concern to God, He graciously received it. He took it from me so that I no longer needed to carry the burden of comparison.

Fixing our eyes on another woman's path—whether it's marriage, social media follows, financial prosperity, idyllic motherhood, career success—is deadly. And it's guaranteed to leave you feeling lifeless. The plan God has for your life necessarily looks drastically different from the plan He has for her life. Because God has a unique path and plan for each one of us, the timing, speed, traveling companions, mission, and destination will all be different! Though stretches of the journey may be similar—if you're called to service, or family, or ministry, or business—the One who has designed you flawlessly, with a unique set of gifts, passions, experiences, and interests, has detailed a plan that only you can accomplish.

And though I struggled with the temptation to compare myself to others, when I was in my right mind I knew that my story was never *meant* to match the stories of the women around me. The plan God had for me was contoured for who God had designed me to be, and He was longing to share the details with me.

THE MOST IMPORTANT QUESTION

I believe God gave me the desire to be married one day. Through the pain of my past relationships, I'd learned the kind of man my heart desired: a man who fully guarded his heart, his mind, and his body. A man who was fully devoted to the Lord. A man who'd be selfless with his life and his time on this earth. A man who'd be a leader, a warrior, a risk taker, and who'd walk closely with the Lord.

And around wedding number sixteen or seventeen, I realized, *The kind of guy I'm looking for is hard to find— nearly impossible!* (Some days I wondered if he even existed!) The thought that came next really challenged me: *If he's so hard to find, what kind of girl is he looking for? He'll want a rarity, too.*

The Lord had been convicting my heart that what I'd longed for—to be chosen, to be loved, to be adored, to be united—was available now, *in Him*. Instead of searching for temporary solutions to fill the void, I set my heart on God. I spent about a year falling in love with Him and discovering His heart for me while allowing Him to heal my heart.

Once I'd shared my most painful questions with God, I could settle in and listen. I dug deep into His Word, studying the life of Jesus. And I continued to lay my life bare before the Lord. He heard the deep cry of my brokenness, and He cared about the pain I was enduring. He and I grew closer together. As I poured out every emotion to the listening ear of the Lord, I began to feel convicted. I realized that in my selfishness, I'd failed to ask God the same questions.

"God, what breaks Your heart?"

As my lips slowed down, the Spirit moved me to tip my ear toward the Lord. "God, You've listened to me. You've heard my cry. It's time I listen to You."

I let God know I was willing and ready to hear Him. "Lord, I will listen if You want to share with me the things that break Your heart."

As I listened closely, He began to speak to me.

THE ORPHANS

To be honest, the orphaned children of the world had never been a concern of mine. They were distant, far away, in a world where I'd never let my mind linger. I'd never met an orphan. I'd never known an orphan. I understood they existed, but they were alien to my world.

Naturally, when the Lord began to speak to my heart about orphans, I did what any millennial would do: I googled it.

When I learned there are over 150 million orphaned children in the world today, I couldn't fathom it. Really, 150 million children? It was more than I could process.

What, Lord? How?

How had I never known this? I'd been blinded to the darkness in the world by the darkness of my own world. The lack in my own life, my broken heart, had consumed me to the neglect of others around the globe who were broken and suffering.

As God spoke to me, my heart began thumping to a new beat. I was on a mission to discover how God wanted me to engage with orphans. It was no idle curiosity, either. I had to find out. I was desperate to know more. And that winter I began reading stories of people who'd done great things for the kingdom.

I studied the stories of biblical leaders like Joshua and Moses.

I read Beth Moore's book *Believing God.*

I read the writings of Mother Teresa and was captured by her sacrificial work among the poorest of the poor in Calcutta.

I read *Radical: Taking Back Your Faith from the American Dream* by David Platt, which challenges comfortable Christians with the way of Jesus, and *Sun Stand Still* by Steven Furtick, about believing impossible prayers. I read everything I could get my hands on, trying to find answers to the questions pulsing in my heart.

I would spend hours at my yogurt store researching and studying everything I could find about orphans and those living in poverty. Day by day, growing a business started to look a lot less exciting than growing the kingdom.

Every page of scripture, every chapter of these books, every quiet whisper from God convinced me of two things:

1. The American "big home with a white picket fence" dream I'd bought into was a hollow one.
2. God saved my life so it could be used for one purpose: to grow His kingdom.

The first one deserves all kinds of disclaimers. It's not a slam on marriage, motherhood, or even beautiful homes with fences. It just means there's something more, even greater, beyond our everyday dreams. It means that God was speaking to my heart and whispering that my dream was too small.

God began to expose everything I'd set my hopes on for what it was. My dream of earthly pleasures and domestic bliss, inspired by my personal agenda, expanded no farther than the property lines of the glamorous lifestyle I'd imagined for myself. My dream was consumed with growing my own treasures on this earth. Yet as I pored over the Gospels, as I listened to the teachings of Jesus, I saw no evidence of the insular kind of dream I'd imagined.

Instead, as I read the scriptures, I saw the heart of Jesus and a beautifully expansive Gospel that was meant to reach the whole world. I saw true Christ followers who sacrificed their own safety and comfort for the sake of others. I began to glimpse a moving picture of life that gives life to others. And through these stories, God whet my appetite to join the work of building Jesus' kingdom.

The "kingdom of Jesus" had always been a little confusing to me. As a girl I'd envisioned a combination of a royal palace and Disney's Magic Kingdom. But now the Lord was revealing fresh truths about His kingdom. Unlike earthly kingdoms built on wealth and status, the Lord's kingdom can't be comprehended by the human mind. Built on heavenly riches, God's kingdom has a divine authority. Under no circumstance can it be shaken. It guarantees our heavenly citizenship. Jesus' kingdom is the place where our hearts dwell, and it's meant to be shared freely, giving life to the lifeless.

Hear me out: partnering with Jesus to usher in the kingdom doesn't preclude romance, marriage, family, or domesticity. But nothing I read in the Gospels suggested that the Christian life was ever meant to be confined within the walls of our homes or the edges of our properties. In fact, I was beginning to see, with fresh eyes, that when Jesus commissioned the disciples to "go into all the world and preach the gospel to all creation" (Mark 16:15), He was not offering a suggestion. He was guiding us into the *only* way to follow Him.

As I was being shaped by these writings, my eyes were being opened to the ways that the American gospel of comfort and pleasure so radically contradicts Jesus' gospel of sacrifice and service. Jesus had sacrificed His life so that I could live; and my living was meant to imitate His, as I gave myself sacrificially to others. He was teaching me that the Gospel is contagious when our lives truly begin to imitate Christ.

GOD'S VISION

If we want to get close to God, we must know what breaks His heart and choose to see what He sees.

He hears the cries of two-thirds of the children of this world who live hungry, searching through the city dumps because their parents cannot afford to feed their tiny malnourished bodies. He sees their suffering, and His heart breaks.

He sees countless little girls sold into the sex trade by mothers deceived by pimps into believing their daughters will receive an education and a better life than the one they could provide. And God's heart breaks.

God sees the rise of Islam spreading through villages and countries around the world and the people He loves believing in false religions, and His heart breaks.

The enemy wants to convince you that the suffering ones are irrelevant, that it's not realistic for you to play a part in changing their story. And his timeless trick is to cloak our minds in darkness by keeping us focused on ourselves—our peers, our feeds, our own bondages—and on the things of the world that actually are irrelevant!

Yet when we finally turn away from our mirrors, phones, personal struggles, and comparisons, the light dawns and we become aware of the purpose we were born to live: going into the darkness to shine with Christ's light.

We are living in dark days. Today more than 27 million people are living in slavery—more today than at any other moment in history. Today more than 150 million children are living on the streets, orphaned, impoverished, and suffering from diseases.[1] This number represents 8.4 percent of all the children in the world and is expected to grow by 20 million every year. Today Islam is the fastest-growing religion in the world and is predicted to surpass Christianity in the decades ahead.

It's a sobering moment when Paul's words to the church in Ephesus ring as true today as they ever have:

You groped your way through that murk once, but no longer. You're out in the open now. The bright light of Christ makes your way plain. So no more stumbling around. Get on with it! The good, the right, the true—these are the actions appropriate for daylight hours. Figure out what will please Christ, and then do it.

Don't waste your time on useless work, mere busywork, the barren pursuits of darkness. Expose these things for the sham they are. It's a scandal when people waste their lives on things they must do in the darkness where no one will see. Rip the cover off those frauds and see how attractive they look in the light of Christ.

> *Wake up from your sleep,*
> *Climb out of your coffins;*
> *Christ will show you the light!*

So watch your step. Use your head. Make the most of every chance you get. These are desperate times! (Ephesians 5:8–16 MSG)

Because I believe God's plan for your life is far greater than your own dreams, I have to ask: Are you sleeping through the greatest moment in history? Knowing we are in desperate times, are you willing to emerge from the darkness and chase after the kingdom?

USE ME

After reading story after story of "crazy, radical Christians" who sold out their lives, I realized God was asking me to make a decision: to pursue my dream of finally living the "normal life" or to pursue the dream God was setting before me. I could continue reading stories about people who chose to step out in faith, believing God could use them to change nations, rescue the vulnerable, and make an impact for His kingdom, *or* I could take the Lord seriously and join them.

God was continuing to soften my spirit for a very particular group of vulnerable ones: *orphans*. It was the word I continued to hear whispered to the ears of my heart.

Yet as quickly as God prompted me, my mind filled with obstacles.

I'd never been on a single mission trip, let alone encountered an orphan.

The loan I'd taken out to start the yogurt shop meant I was in debt over my head.

I couldn't see where I'd begin to carve out the time. I was running a business. I was deeply invested in my church. I led kids in my church every weekend. I had an active friend group. I was studying scripture voraciously, reading and rereading the words of Jesus in the Gospels.

But I wanted nothing more than to be faithful.

Without having any idea what it meant or where it would lead, I breathed a prayer of response to God.

"Okay, I'll do it. I'll help orphans."

Chapter 7

WHEN GOD SPEAKS

God invites us to walk out His plan with others.

After wedding season, I celebrated finishing college by attending the Passion Conference in Atlanta alongside about forty thousand other young people between the ages of eighteen and twenty-five. The annual gathering was keynoted that year by amazing speakers like Christine Caine, Francis Chan, and John Piper. Throughout the three-day gathering, these leaders challenged us to offer our lives to God to be used for what matters most.

During worship, I was in my seat in the Georgia Dome, praying fervently about God's call on my life to serve orphans.

"God," I begged, "show me one more time, and I'll go all in."

I can hear how those sound just like the words that someone resisting God's call would say! But God knew my heart. God knew I longed, more than anything, to be sold out to His mission; I just needed His green light.

As I opened my eyes, about forty children were marching single file onto the stage. They looked like they were of African descent. As I heard the conference band begin to play, I couldn't believe what my ears were hearing. The gentle opening rhythm of Chris Tomlin's song "How Great Is Our God."

It was the song I'd sung in the hospital as a girl with my mom. It was the one I'd listened to before each surgery.

And though these beautiful children sang it in their native tongue, I heard it in my own.

I scrambled to open the conference guide and learned that these beloved ones who were singing my song were all *orphans* from Uganda.

I melted.

I knew God was speaking to me, but it wasn't clear what He was saying.

After the song, Francis Chan spoke and then sent us to our smaller groups that were scattered nearby.

Stepping outside the Georgia Dome, heading for my small-group session, I felt a bitter cold wind slap my face. Shivering, I went in search of my group meeting space at a nearby facility. We'd been sent out in a moment of silence in which we were to reflect on the reality of human trafficking. I wasn't exactly sure where we were meeting, and because of the silence I felt like I couldn't ask. Freezing, still praying, I ended up lost and scared in downtown Atlanta.

Glancing at my watch, I became upset when I realized I'd lost about twenty minutes wandering in search of the meeting spot. As I prayed and listened for God to speak to me, I heard His strong voice as clearly as I'd ever heard it before.

"I will use you to change the world."

What?

It wasn't an audible voice, but God's message impressed itself on my heart with a spiritual authority I'd never before encountered.

My impulse was to write it down so I wouldn't forget, but my hands were too cold to function well. The eight words were so powerful, though, that I knew they'd stay with me.

And they did.

I finally found the meeting location, but instead of looking for my small group, I stayed in the lobby. After rubbing my hands back to warmth and life, I grabbed a pen and wrote in my journal the words that God had spoken to me.

"Yes, Lord. I will go."

GOD'S GREEN LIGHT

Apparently that was all God needed—a willing heart.

When God had spoken to me before about the direction He had for me, I tended to offer Him my list of disqualifications, my inabilities, and my lack of resources. If I'm completely honest, I offered Him my excuses. And let's get real: my handicaps meant I had more disqualifications than the average person!

I was twenty-three, single, and buried in debt. But God spoke plainly to me: *"There are only two traits that you must possess if you want to be used by Me: willingness and obedience."*

God uses the willing and the obedient.

Assuring me that none of my objections had disqualified me, the Lord began to show me the vast resources He'd entrusted to me. I had a supportive family. I had a wide network of friends. I had a store that served over two hundred customers every day.

Wanting to begin moving in the direction God had already given me, still unclear about what this journey would actually look like, one afternoon I called my Orange Leaf staff together.

"Hey, guys," I began, "I want to share with you something that God's been doing in my heart." Six faces waited to hear what I would share.

I continued, "Lately God's been showing me how much He loves the neglected children around the world and how important it is that we care for them. It's the least we can do with how much we have been given."

I knew some, though not all, of my crew were committed believers.

"I think it's time that we have a bigger vision than just serving yogurt," I explained. "I believe God can use a little yogurt shop to change the world. "

Eyebrows rose. I thought I saw some enthusiasm in their faces.

"We serve a lot of people in here each day, and we have an opportunity to impact the lives of all our customers," I continued. "But what if we did something greater than that? What if we mobilized our customers to impact the lives of others?"

They still looked like they were tracking with me.

"Starting today, we, as a team, are going to build a home for orphaned children."

Our shop was adjacent to Oral Roberts University. That meant we saw a lot of students and we also served a lot of moms and families with kids in private schools. I felt certain they would embrace our mission. So we started selling items in the store to raise awareness. We sold red T-shirts with "Love" printed in turquoise ink over the continent of Africa. We sold orange leather bracelets engraved with the words "Love Never Fails."

When I was in the shop, I welcomed opportunities to tell curious customers what we were up to and how the sales would benefit orphans in need of a loving home. And it was awesome to see my staff get on board, too. They quickly became enthusiastic ambassadors raising funds for the sake of orphaned children they had never met.

As we were raising money, I continued researching everything I could about caring for orphaned children.

FAITHFUL GUIDES

I'd been attending a Bible study at the home of Debbie and Ron, a couple at my church who were about the age of my parents. They opened their home every Tuesday night, serving dinner to anyone in my generation who'd come. After dinner the guys would meet with Ron in the living room, and the girls would go to an upstairs living room with Debbie.

A deeper hunger was brewing in me. Eager to learn and grow, I wanted to use the time I had as a single woman, as one fixing to launch on the mission God had for me, to prepare myself for what was coming. As I saw my friends getting married, and now a few even beginning to have children, I felt strongly that this season of my life was a gift. And though God was faithful to meet me in His Word and in prayer and through the group at Debbie and Ron's, I also wanted to reap the deeper wisdom of women who were a few years further along in their walk than I was.

The two women I approached were Debbie and Rachel.

"Teach me everything you know," I told them.

Debbie was an amazing example of a godly woman. I knew she'd mentored another girl I admired named Rachel, who was about five years older than me. With a mingling of hesitance and boldness, I asked Debbie and Rachel if they'd consider mentoring me. Graciously, they agreed. We met every three weeks throughout the year. I wanted to seek God's will for me and for the world. And doing it in the presence of these godly women, one who was a few steps ahead of me and the other who was about fourteen steps ahead of me, was an amazing gift. These two women taught me how to study the Bible differently. We studied the disciplines of the Bible—like fasting, meditation, and prayer—together. As we shared our lives, we were being formed by the disciplines that shaped Jesus and believers throughout the centuries. My time with them was like a breath of fresh air.

Debbie and Rachel loved God and loved me. They listened deeply to the stirrings of my heart. They dug into God's Word with me. They spoke truth and blessings over me. They also prepared me to say yes when I'd eventually have the opportunity to mentor and invest in girls younger than me.

My friends and I tend to refer to the leading spiritual ladies in our lives as our "girl gang." There will always be those girls in our lives who are wonderful friends with whom we can shop, grab coffee, or do brunch. But there are also those girls in our lives who go beyond the call of duty to pray together, fast together, and intervene on our behalf. These are the ladies you want in your corner. These are the ones who will sharpen you, challenge you, support you, and encourage you. This is your girl gang! The coolest thing about coming to know Jesus more deeply is that you begin to attract women who are as crazy and radical as you are.

Maybe your spiritual appetite has been whet, like mine was, to grow in the Lord. That desire is itself a gift from God. I encourage you to seek out godly women who can walk with you as you open your life to the Lord and to them. Because I've known a lot of girls who would have loved to have had these relationships in their lives, but for a variety of reasons did not, I encourage you to be intentional—and maybe even a little bold!—as you seek out women to share your journey. Really, those are the two criteria: loving God and loving you.

During the season that I spent with Debbie and Rachel, I began to sense that God was leading me to travel eight thousand miles from home. Before I ever breathed a word to anyone else, I asked Debbie and Rachel to hold the possibility in their hearts and pray over the opportunity with me.

CLOSE TO GOD

The sweet season that the Lord had invited me into at the beginning of my senior year in college continued beyond graduation, through eighteen weddings, and into the next year. When I'd expected to feel most alone—as friends moved on from college—I was often aware of the Lord's presence with me. Of course I "felt" it in prayer and as God spoke to me through His Word, but I was also aware, as I worked at the store or trained at the gym, that God genuinely cared about every need and desire of my heart.

After graduation I'd come home to live in Tulsa. Gentry was attending the University of Oklahoma School of Law. When she came home, we'd hang out on my bed like little girls at a sleepover party and share the deepest parts of our hearts with each other.

My bed was made of cherrywood and the comforter was cream. Framed pictures crowned my dresser. One was of my whole family at Bradley's high school graduation. There was a picture of my cousin Rachel and me at Myrtle Beach when we were kids. In a picture of Lauren and me at our Chi O '80s prom costume party, our huge hair, party shades, and neon dresses screamed sorority life. But a few pictures were missing. Though the void never would have been caught by a stranger passing through my bedroom—a plumber or a carpet cleaner—there were no pictures of me from the day of my stroke through the next three years. It's not that I chose not to display them, either. It's that I didn't allow them to be taken. For the three years that I'd felt like a stranger in my own skin, when the girl I saw in the mirror failed to match the one I knew myself to be, I'd been determined to avoid being photographed. My friends caught on pretty quickly and respected my space. My family, too. But when certain events, like a family wedding, required a group shot, I'd smile and tip my right side to the camera.

One weekend after shopping with my mom, Gentry wandered into my room and sat on my bed. Glad for the company, I continued to hang up clothes while we chatted.

"Hey, what's up?" she asked.

My heart was full with something I wanted to share with her. God had finally shown me the first step in the journey we were embarking on together.

I began cautiously, "Well, you know how the Lord's been speaking to me about orphans?"

I'd learned there were millions of orphans in Africa. The problem was so huge. And these children were just as precious as I was to the Lord. For the six months the

Lord had been pressing orphans on my heart, I hadn't known what God wanted me to do. I hadn't known where to start. I hadn't known what engagement would look like. I wasn't reluctant to respond—I was waiting for God to show me what to do.

"Yeah. . ." she answered, her voice rising slightly in pitch.

Though my back was to her as I was hanging up clothes, I heard a spark of interest and delight in her voice.

Gentry knew I was raising money for orphans. It wasn't a secret. At Orange Leaf, we were already engaging our customers in the effort to help children. But I knew that even more could be done.

Over the winter I'd begun approaching Tulsa business owners, inviting them to partner with me. I would produce discount cards, which I'd sell for ten dollars each, that would give customers one dollar off a product or service each Wednesday for the rest of the year. Forty local businesses, including Wolfgang Puck, Supercuts, and others, participated in the fund-raiser.

When I paused before continuing, Gentry pressed, "Come on, girl. Spill it. What's going on?"

Gentry knew that whatever I was about to say, wherever I sensed the Lord was leading, was a train that was probably pretty far down the track. I'm not the kind of person who throws out twenty ideas and hopes one of them sticks. The Lord knows I'm a questioner, and when God does speak to me, I ask Him to reaffirm it for me *several* times! By the time I speak it out loud, by the time I share it with someone else, it's no longer a wondering or a maybe: it has become a matter of fact.

"Well," I said, setting down the clothes I was holding

and joining her on the bed, "I found this organization that's going to Uganda. You know that country I told you about?"

She nodded.

"I found an organization from Tulsa that's going to Uganda. I think I told you I wanted to raise money for them, but now I'm thinking I might want to go."

For the fund-raising we'd been doing at Orange Leaf and in the business community, I'd set a goal to build an orphan home in Uganda.

"Ooh, I wanna go with you!" Gentry exploded. "How can I help? What can I do?"

I laughed at her excitement, though I wasn't surprised. She jumped up off the bed as we brainstormed together.

"The timing is perfect," she gushed. "I take the bar in June and get sworn in come September!"

Her enthusiasm was contagious. I'd spent the last ten weeks since the Passion Conference researching orphan care. Learning about Uganda. Discovering the many ways people were caring for orphans around the globe. I'd done my homework, and I was ready! I showed her the ministry online and we began to talk about what our trip might look like. Confident God was leading us both, we were psyched about the trip.

SHARING

That night at the dinner table, as we enjoyed my mom's delicious fried chicken, our parents' reaction was a bit less enthusiastic than Gentry's.

"Uganda—you want to go to Uganda?" my dad asked. It wasn't so much a question as incredulous bafflement.

Having anticipated this very reaction, I'd been laying the groundwork for months. Though I hadn't known exactly where the Lord's guiding hand would lead, I'd been confident enough that God was inviting me into an adventure with Him to impact the world for His kingdom that I'd been dropping bread crumbs for my parents to track.

First, I'd let them know I was growing closer to God, the living God, in scripture and in prayer. Both of them were delighted and supportive.

Then I'd shared with them that God had been speaking to me about helping orphans. That seemed honorable enough. Inarguable.

Later I looped them in when God invited me to help orphans in *Uganda*. They knew I'd been doing fund-raising at the store and around Tulsa. Anyone, even my father the skilled attorney, would have a hard time protesting that one.

It wasn't accidental that I'd chosen that night to tell them I was planning to travel to Uganda. I suspected I'd need Gentry's support, and their reactions at the table proved it.

"Honey," my mom protested, concern in her voice, "is your body up for a trip like this?"

And that was the real scare.

They had devoted the last dozen years of their lives to getting me well and couldn't, in good conscience, send a sick child to a land reputed for deadly diseases. They had known various missionaries who'd returned from the continent with malaria, typhoid, and other diseases. Their understanding of the corruption in Africa also caused them to believe that something very serious could happen there. Specifically, they were afraid that with all the uncontrolled variables of overseas travel and unpredictable accommodations in a third-world country, my body would be more vulnerable to getting sick. It was what they'd spent years fighting to rescue me from.

"Mom," Gentry countered, "I'll go with her, and if anything happens, I'll make sure she is okay!"

I read my parents' faces and could see that her offer gave them little comfort.

"It's not for another nine months," I reasoned, "and we have all the time in the world to prepare."

We bantered back and forth for much of the meal, my parents expressing their concerns and Gentry and I assuring them it would all work out fine. I suppose it wasn't unlike the conversations many adult children in their early twenties have with parents who are pushing fifty. The difference, of course, was how close this "child" had once been to death.

Convinced that I was responding to God's call, I was unwilling to back down.

"I'm going on this trip," I announced definitively. "The Lord's telling me to do it, so I'm going."

And with that, I left the room. I knew it was rude, but I was convinced I was in the right.

Because my parents had always supported missionaries around the world, my argument that God was sending me wasn't an easy one to refute. The next morning I apologized to my mom.

Recognizing that she and my dad were probably beat, my mom finally conceded, speaking for herself and my dad: "Well, we're really going to need to pray about it."

Confident God wouldn't give her a different answer than I'd heard, that worked for me.

DISCERNING YOUR PURPOSE

I'm convinced that God has a plan for each one of us to change the world and that His plan is *knowable*. We don't accidentally discover God's plan. It doesn't just show up in our mailboxes. Receiving God's will for our lives depends on our willingness to listen. I am not more special than you or the next girl at the coffee shop, but I did make the choice to listen.

You can, too.

Jesus assures us, "Whoever belongs to God hears what God says" (John 8:47). God wants nothing more than to make His voice clear to you as you listen.

In the book *Forever Ruined for the Ordinary*, author Joy Dawson offers guidance on hearing the voice of God by suggesting the different ways God speaks to us: through His Word; via the daily reading of the Bible; through what we see; through dreams, visions, angels, consuming fire, and natural signs; and through special kinds of hearing.

Dawson encourages, "The voice of the Lord is quiet but persistent." And she adds, "When God speaks into our minds, His voice is inaudible to our outer ears, but clear to the inner ear of our spirits."[2]

Hearing God's voice is one of the most intimate benefits of having a relationship with a living God. He wants to speak to you and tell you secrets about yourself, your future, and what He has called you to do with your life. If you want to hear God's voice, you must listen. Get alone. Get quiet. And ask the Lord to silence any voices that are not from Him. As you wait and listen, He will speak. If you will seek, He will speak.

When the Lord told me He would use me to change

the world, the voice I heard was in my inner ear, in my spirit. It was quiet and confirmed what He was already speaking to me. He offered the words "I will use you to change the world" as more of an invitation than a command. I could almost hear God follow the announcement with, "Are you willing? Are you ready?"

The Lord wants to use you to change the world, too. There is no gifting, ability, qualification, license, skill, financial state, or resource you need. The only thing He asks for is a willing and obedient heart.

Are you ready to be used by the Lord?

Before you agree, be careful. Asking to be used by God is a dangerous prayer. It changes the way you think, the way you view life, and the way you view others. It's a prayer that changes everything.

If you have a longing in your heart right now for something more than the life you have been living, and you don't know where to start looking for answers, begin by studying the life of Jesus. There's no way to follow Him if you're not thoroughly acquainted with the way He lived. Notice whom He spoke to and how He spoke to them. Pay attention to His heart and what mattered most to Him. In what did He invest His energy, and in what did He not invest His energy? Knowing Jesus intimately is the secret to living a life that matters.

WALKING OUT GOD'S PLAN WITH OTHERS

Can you recognize the rich network of people who helped shape my clear sense of mission and purpose? On one hand, I'm most interested in getting my final directions directly from God. On the other hand, I'm also aware that God gives us other women to grow and teach and lead us. Having the right women in your corner to offer sound advice and to support you along the journey can be life changing.

Perhaps you're already embedded in an awesome community that is eager to help you discover where God is leading you. Or maybe you're feeling more alone on your journey to serve God and the ones He loves. I'm convinced it is God's good pleasure for us to serve Him with the love, prayer, and support of others.

Community is a gift God loves to give. And give abundantly.

Chapter 8

MY COMFORTS EXPOSED

God exposes our privilege to move us to respond to pain.

Before I stepped out in faith, I wanted to recognize God's clear leading. I wanted to know *who*. I wanted to know *where*. I wanted to know *when*. I wanted to know *how*.

I was still confident about the "who": orphans. And the Lord had been enlarging my heart to love the children in Uganda who'd been orphaned.

Because I still didn't see the big picture, I was stepping forward with what I did know by visiting a ministry in Uganda with Gentry.

THE JOURNEY

We left on December 15th, and the flights were brutally long! We flew with a team of six from Tulsa—two hours to Chicago, then eight to Amsterdam, then eight and a half more to Kigali, and then one more to Entebbe. By the time we arrived, I had no idea how long we'd been gone or what time it even would have been in Tulsa.

Because Gentry and I were both picky eaters—in America, before we'd ever traveled around the globe to a new culture!—we did our homework and packed an entire suitcase full of trail mix, protein bars, goldfish crackers, and meal replacement bars. And because my doctors and my parents hadn't wanted me to travel to Africa in the first place, so far from the reliable care on which I'd grown to depend, I'd stocked up on all the medications I'd need and promised to be vigilant about taking them. Naive about where we were going, Gentry and I even packed baby outfits that we bought at a Tulsa boutique, backup phone chargers in hopes of the possibility that we might have Internet access, and a few cute dresses we'd ordered online for the trip. I'd even packed bottles of water so I could control every single thing that went into my body.

When we arrived in Entebbe, a driver was holding a sign that had the name of the organization on it. As we watched the luggage coming off our flight spin around on the conveyor belt, we didn't immediately spot ours. When the last bag was picked up and the belt ground to a halt, our bags were nowhere to be seen. After speaking with airline representatives, we discovered that our bags hadn't been on the flight and the next flight originating in Amsterdam wasn't coming in for two more days.

No familiar foods.

No water bottled in America.

No vitamins.

No clothes.

I'd packed the antimalarial pills in my purse. Unfortunately, the side effects from the medication were dangerous to people, like me, who have epilepsy. To counteract those ill effects, I'd packed vitamins and probiotics in the suitcase that never arrived. And what I most needed, since it wouldn't be available in the rural village we'd be visiting, was a case of water I'd also packed.

Had the ministry been located in the neighborhood of Kampala, we might have dashed back to the airport in a couple of days to fetch our bags. But the driver was taking us on an eight-hour trip, over rugged bumpy rural roads, to reach our destination. Without food, water, supplements, or extra clothing, Gentry and I had no choice but to fake like it was no big deal and get in the van and continue on.

EYES OPENED

Before that van ride, I would have told you that I'd seen poverty before. When we'd vacationed in the Bahamas or St. Thomas, we'd passed slum neighborhoods on the way to dine at a restaurant or visit a beach. But as we bumped along on our journey, I realized I had no category for the breadth and depth of need I was witnessing. Though there were often vast scenic stretches of gorgeous countryside, we also drove through miles and miles of towns and villages screaming with need. Shoeless young children dressed in rags, mostly unsupervised, stood precariously close to the unpredictable road. Thin, frail mothers tried to care for lifeless infants. Stick-built homes masqueraded as shelter. This wasn't a pocket of a town or city. It was sprawling poverty to which I could see no end.

The radical difference between my own comfortable childhood (and the childhoods of most everyone I'd ever known) and the tragic experiences of so many Ugandan children was unnerving. On a planet that presumably has enough resources for us all, I struggled to make sense of the massive gap in resources between these precious children without enough, and those in my world who had access to plenty.

When we arrived in Mabaale, children flocked to our minivan, begging to be held. Before I could step out of the van, a precious baby girl was holding on to my leg.

Admittedly, eight very light-skinned people were an oddity in rural Uganda! But I felt like I was witnessing something more than an interest in the rarity of our complexions.

Though the organization had been started by Americans, they'd wisely partnered with a local pastor. Sarah, the pastor's wife, met us and led us to a guesthouse where Gentry and I shared a room. Wary of the flimsy building's proximity to nature, I surveyed the open windows and gates for doors.

Cautious, desperately hoping the answer would be no, I asked Sarah, "Are there any snakes?"

"Yes," she confirmed in a thick, beautiful Ugandan accent, nodding her head. "I have killed many cobras in this house where you are standing."

Mortified, I forced a polite smile.

"When was the last time you killed one?" I asked, hoping her answer would be measured in years. Or decades.

"Yesterday," she said proudly, as if her service would comfort me.

What I felt inside was quite the opposite of comfort.

Though I was grateful the previous day's threat met his end, the proximity of the threat still disturbed me.

Though I would have loved to have bathed and changed clothes after our epic travel relay, I had nothing to wear but the colorful sleeveless dress in which I'd traveled. Splashing some water on my face, while praying it didn't touch my lips, I stepped back outside to meet more children in the center of the ministry's property.

The sun had begun to set as Gentry and I walked toward the center of the property. Children pressed against us, raising their thin, ashy arms to be lifted and held. Desperate for human touch and affection, they had such need in their eyes. Many behaved as if they felt ill. Moving at a slower pace, they appeared to be sick. Their eyes were runny and red, their noses dripping, their little bodies radiating heat.

When one of the children spotted a large, dangerous green mamba snake in the adjacent field, the children—suddenly vivified!—all ran toward the danger, throwing rocks at the snake. The sight triggered a memory of being at a park as a child with my mom and Gentry. When a little boy spotted a garter snake, Gentry and I both ran from the snake, squealing, into our mother's waiting arms. Yet these children had not learned to flee from danger to the safety of reliable caregivers but, in the absence of reliable caregivers, had learned to run *toward* a threat, attacking it. When the snake had been pelted by 360 degrees of rocks and stones, it was eventually disoriented enough that one of the older children came close enough to begin beating it with a heavy tree branch. The scene was an apt snapshot of the lives of vulnerable children left largely to defend themselves.

As shocking as it was to see children chasing snakes, it was just as awful to see a child who was barely three with a machete larger than his body in his hands. He was cutting grass with it in an open field.

Despite the fiercely beautiful children, I felt the heavy burden of darkness throughout my visit. As I prayed about what I was experiencing, I came to believe that God's Spirit had allowed me to recognize a lingering spirit of oppression. That recognition signaled to me that God's light was needed desperately in this world where basic physical need bled into the spiritual realm.

Another day during my visit, as I cradled two young twin girls in my lap, I was reminded of a story that I'd heard the day before about the siblings. The two girls and their younger brother had witnessed their mother being murdered and, since that tragic day, were left with no choice but to fend for themselves.

Now, holding them in my lap and watching boys carve pictures in the dirt with rocks, I was made more aware of my privilege. And I begged God to show me how the two worlds—my privileged one and the desperate reality of orphans—might collide in such a way that God would be glorified as the children He loved were blessed.

Though I had a world of respect for what the ministry was doing, it was difficult to observe the overwhelming emotional neediness of the children and believe that their deep needs were being met.

NEED UPON NEED

Before bed, I took a quick cold bath, standing in a bucket that had been provided for our use, and slipped out of my dress. Without pajamas, I slept in a T-shirt that a girl I was traveling with let me borrow. I climbed into a bed that had been covered with a mosquito net and pulled a light sheet over myself. That first night my mind was going a million miles an hour, and I had a hard time sleeping. Lying awake in bed, I had to pinch myself to believe it was true. The scent of the evening's wood fire lingered on my dress that lay beside the bed. African insects chirped from nearby woods. The air was heavy with humidity. Determined to keep my head in the right place, I pushed thoughts of snakes and spiders from my mind.

What seemed most absurd was that I was in Uganda! Mind still racing, I finally drifted off to sleep after a few hours.

The next morning, just as darkness broke, our alarm clock was the crowing of an enthusiastic rooster! Gentry and I, slipping back into our dresses, got ready for the day and settled into a quiet time with the Lord. (By "got ready," I mean we got out of bed. We still didn't have a toothbrush, face wash, face cream, or anything else.) When a bell rang at seven, we joined the rest of our group for breakfast.

School was out for vacation, which meant we were with the children 24-7! While I think some visitors could have handled the constant clamoring with ease, it was really exhausting for me. Naturally wired as an introvert, I'm refueled by the time I have in solitude: reading, praying, studying, remaining silent. So the incessant cry for attention of young voices and clawing touch really drained me. I felt like it exposed my heart to needs even greater than the children's physical ones, like the need to feel loved and bonded to an adult. Throughout the week, large groups of sick little children would follow us around. As soon as we would set a child down, three more would line up to be held.

MY COMFORTS, THEIR NEEDS

Almost half of Uganda's 2.5 million orphans have been orphaned by AIDS.[3] And while there was no way for me to wrap my mind around a number like 2.5 million, I did bear witness to the desperate number of orphaned children when we toured the area to see other local ministries and orphanages. Many of the children we saw were malnourished and sick. Some had no clothes to wear. Most lacked nutritious foods. Without access to safe water sources, children would bathe in whatever water source they could find. Some children even worked long days as slaves just to have a meal. Throughout the week, my eyes were opened to the enormity of the world's orphan crisis.

I knew that various mission agencies had different approaches to running trips like these. Some sought to provide the most comfortable accommodations so that visitors wouldn't be distracted from what they'd come to discover by discomfort—so that they wouldn't risk missing the meaning of the trip. That, however, wasn't what I experienced. In fact, the week was a radical departure from the comforts I'd always taken for granted. The colorful dress I'd worn on the plane, racer-backed, scoop-necked, ankle-length, was my constant companion. I'd loved it when I ordered it online in Tulsa but had grown to despise it by the middle of the week. In most moments, I was dripping hot, salty sweat. The sweat, of course, served as an adhesive for dust and dirt to cling to my warm flesh. In the evenings I'd bathe in a bucket of cold water. While that might sound refreshing, in the wake of a heat-scorched day, the experience was actually jarring.

My temporary discomforts only highlighted the daily life of the children who had no way to escape the same obstacles. If a child had a T-shirt and shorts, or a skirt, he or she would wear the same torn, dirty clothes every day. Their baths were infrequent, and they had to drink the water that was pulsing with bacteria that I was nervous to even bathe with. In the absence of my protein bars, I'd been forced to depend on local food. Our hosts were wildly generous in serving their guests, and I knew the children in the orphanage would have loved to have access, as we did, to all the food they wanted and needed. Even the chicken leg that made me feel a little queasy would have been a rare delicacy for the children in the orphanage, who were fed chicken only on Christmas Day.

I'd read about rich people in the Bible, but until I visited rural Uganda, I'd never considered myself to be one. The kinds of rich people Jesus seemed to take issue with were the ones who built extra barns to store their wealth, who actively oppressed the poor, and who refused to do justice. I'd never considered myself "rich." After all, I was over a hundred thousand dollars in debt with my Orange Leaf business!

And yet, throughout the week, God opened my eyes to my privilege and to my priorities. As God exposed the priorities I'd clung to for so many years—falling in love, building a career, growing a family, enjoying a lifestyle of ease—I realized I wasn't so different from the rich man who missed the kingdom of God because his focus was on things that didn't really matter.

That growing awareness was like a cold bath that shocked me to my senses.

Yes, I'd been excited to help children, but being in Uganda had exposed the deeper issues of my heart. Comforts stripped away, I was forced to face the undeniable reality that God was continuing to mold my heart to desire what His own heart desired. Jesus calls us to the weak and the vulnerable, the hurting and the oppressed.

He calls us to be a light in the dark places around the world. Suddenly I had to face how I had called myself a follower of Christ for twenty-four years yet had taken no interest in actually following His lead to care for those in need.

"God," I breathed as I fell off to sleep on our last night in the village, "reshape my heart. Teach me how to truly follow You."

DOING IT BETTER

During our visit, I couldn't turn off the "business" part of my brain. When I noticed inefficient systems, I wanted to see things done differently! At the same time, I certainly understood Americans' temptation to impose our ideas for change onto other cultures, and I did want to guard against arrogant intrusion. But I couldn't help but wish for better systems in place to serve the children more effectively.

For instance, one organization was trying to build a conference center, but I knew that the church building on their own campus, which was *empty* Monday through Saturday, could have been better utilized.

I also saw the way that handouts—such as used American clothing that gets donated to struggling populations—damaged the local economy. And the only way to break poverty in a community is by supporting the local economy.

But my biggest concern was for the flourishing of children. Too often I saw large groups of unsupervised children. And instead of turning to their part-time nannies for nurture or comfort, when these women might be working nearby washing clothes or doing other chores for the twenty-five children they were respon-sible for, the children sought affection from strangers, like those on our team. While I could see the children's lavish attention was heartwarming for some, making them feel wanted and needed, the excessiveness of it raised caution about a need in their life that was still unmet.

I even felt the setup of the homes could be im-proved. The dormitory-style living was designed to care for as many children at once with a long wing that included bedrooms and a bathroom. But the children needed to walk a distance to a community area to eat. While that makes sense for college students, it made less sense for children in need of family bonding with a predictable, stable home environment. Family is a key factor in children's well-being, as a place where children can belong and discover their true identity.

While I was happy these children had access to three slim meals a day, and grateful they weren't being used as house slaves or rented out by pimps, I still didn't have a peace in my heart about the care they were receiving. The emotional neediness of so many convinced me there was something these kids were still missing, and it raised an opportunity for a different approach to orphan care.

As Gentry and I boarded our first flight toward Tulsa, out of Entebbe, I whispered a prayer to God, letting Him know I was willing to rearrange my comfortable life in Tulsa so He could use me to improve the condition of these orphans' lives.

FOLLOWING

My mind had been sold out to *my* future: my future lifestyle, my future family, my future finances. My. My. My. And yet as I continued to study the person of Jesus, I realized that He was sold out to other people. He was available to them. He sacrificed for them. He provided for them. He traveled to them. Unconcerned with social status, He moved among the poor and broken and hurting. He was love covered with flesh.

And the Spirit began teaching me a powerful lesson: You can't be a follower of Christ unless you're actually following Christ. I know that seems obvious, but that reality was transforming me as it made its way into my bones. I'd been a "good" girl who'd lived an upright life. But not actively committing sin didn't mean I'd been actively following Jesus. The Spirit was opening my eyes to the difference between making "good" decisions for my life and making "God" ones. As God transformed me, I began to lose my taste for the first and started hungering for the second.

Believers in the early church were not called "Christians." But they were eventually called Christians by observers who started noticing this group of people whose lives mirrored Christ's life. Following Christ meant spending my time, money, and energy in places I never dreamed I'd be. It meant refusing to live for myself in order to be devoted to a life that was about the needs of others. It meant sacrificing my own dreams for God's greater plan.

I think it's natural to want to know where Christ is leading us. But our tendency to want to know all of the details eliminates our dependency on Him every step of the way.

That's why He might show us where we'll be about

ten steps down the road, then invite us to trust Him for the next nine steps it takes to get there.

God is inviting you to trust Him as His plan for your life unfolds before your eyes.

CHAPTER 9

ORPHAN RAVE

God calls you to serve Him where you are.

"Golf tournament?" she offered. "Maybe a golf tournament?"

God was showing me how best to serve orphans, and I was working alongside two young women, Amy and Kayla. We were at Starbucks, conspiring about how we could raise money for orphan care.

"Mmm. . . ," I responded, weighing her suggestion. "It's a good idea, but I think it would lean toward an older crowd."

We both wanted to mobilize young people, energizing them for this important work.

"You're right," Kayla agreed. "A race? Should we host a race? Like a 5K?"

"That's a good one," I said, noting it in the document where we'd been recording our genius ideas.

"It might be fun to give it some kind of twist. Like. . .those runs with colored dust that bursts everywhere, or—"

Before I could finish my sentence, the perfect idea fell right from heaven into my consciousness.

"I've got it!" I exploded. My clumsy left arm knocked over what was left of my iced chai latte. A little brown stream trickled out onto the table.

"Did you hear about that hunger rave about six months ago?" I asked.

Before Gentry and I had traveled to Uganda, a teenage

boy in Tulsa had hosted a rave to raise money to fight hunger.

If you haven't been to a rave, it's basically an epileptic's nightmare waiting to happen.

It's a five-hour dance party, usually with a DJ blaring music with a loud bass line. The room is dark, with strobe and laser lights everywhere. And by dance party, I mean everyone jumps up and down for hours. A spontaneous rave might spring up at an abandoned warehouse and be spread by word of mouth. Though this one had been clean, a lot of raves are known for drug use and heavy drinking.

"Yeah," Amy confirmed, "I remember that. We should reach out to the kid who did it. I think he went to Metro Christian."

The hunger rave, at the Spirit Event Center, had been an alcohol-free, drug-free event that Tulsa teens had eaten up. A lot of kids from private Christian schools, like the one the organizer attended, had gone to the event.

"Yeah," I added, "my brother went, too! He said it was awesome. And I think it was like ten bucks a ticket."

Kayla's eyes widened. "How many kids do you think we could get?"

"I don't know," I mused. "Seems like if we combined our networks, maybe. . .two-fifty or three hundred? I think my brother could help."

Now we were on a roll.

"Ooh!" I added. "We could sell T-shirts, too. Water, soda, snacks. . . I think we could probably make about three or four thousand bucks in one night!"

And with the spill of a coffee cup, a rave was born.

ORPHAN RAVE

We first tweeted about the April 4 event in January: "We are created to live this life with as much passion as possible!" The tweet linked to online ticket sales.

In January and February tickets were just five dollars. And we gave away glow-in-the-dark #orphanrave bracelets with each ticket sold. By March, tickets were eight dollars online and ten at the door. We put posters up at schools all over the city with our logo that announced, "Live, Love, Rave!"

In addition to tickets, we were selling T-shirts in advance. We printed bright blue tank tops with "RAVE" in orange lettering, and also ones with "Live, Love, Rave" in white lettering. We'd even solicited donations from about eight sponsors and printed their logos on the back of the shirts.

A lot of volunteers helped us push ticket and T-shirt sales. Orange Leaf, where we sold tickets and T-shirts, was sort of our headquarters. We would send the public to the store to purchase their tickets for the event. Bradley and his friends started selling tickets and T-shirts at Jenks' Fellowship of Christian Athletes meetings. Other students would sell tickets at school. When we'd enlist young volunteers, we'd give them thirty tickets in a zipped bank bag, and they'd come back a week later and hand us a bag of money. Some had sold shirts, too, so when they turned in their money they'd get the shirts from Orange Leaf and take them back to the buyers at school.

Bradley had enlisted some great kids at Jenks to help us. The president of the senior class was one of them. He and a friend made a video at Orange Leaf, inviting students to the rave, telling students to find him at school to buy a ticket. Violating school policy by selling tickets at school, he sold about two hundred tickets and T-shirts on campus before the administration finally threatened to rescind his invitation to speak at graduation if he continued. He continued promoting the event, but not on campus.

KHITS, a secular Tulsa radio station, also started promoting the rave.

As anticipation for the April 4 event grew on social media, the word about #orphanrave continued to spread.

THE BIG DAY

While we were glad that students were psyched about the event, a few days before it happened, we started to get a little nervous. We'd presold about five hundred tickets, but we didn't know how many would show up at the door. The buzz on social media was growing, and it was hard to know how many people to anticipate.

One enthusiastic young man who bought a ticket tweeted, "Let's all get wasted for this charity event."

Yeah, that fed our concerns.

Although our posts and posters emphasized that the Orphan Rave was going to be a clean event, it was going to get crazy enough with noise and flashing lights and adrenaline. The last thing we needed was alcohol or drugs. Our first concern was keeping kids safe. But we also wanted the event to breed confidence in our efforts to help orphans. It was hard to see how inebriated minors would do that. We prayed God's protection over the whole evening.

The morning of the event, a team of volunteers started setting up at eight o'clock. We enjoyed a fun day together as we prepared to welcome students, sell T-shirts, check coats, show a few videos about the orphan crisis, and host some giveaways.

The event was scheduled from eight to midnight, and teens started coming around seven thirty. KHITS was broadcasting live outside as students flooded from the parking lot into the venue. (When the numbers began rising higher than we'd anticipated, I was tempted to beg KHITS to stop inviting more teens on air!) We'd hired eight security guards, who checked bags at the door. After passing through security, kids' hands were stamped with our logo. In the foyer, students could buy T-shirts or pay one dollar to check their belongings for the night.

A few of the girls were showing up in very minimal clothing. Some of the shorts were *alarmingly* short, and many tops were cropped short, too. And because we knew that kids would be posting pictures of the event throughout the night, we felt like their risqué choices would reflect poorly on the event and what we were trying to do. In the most extreme cases, we'd hand a girl a blue RAVE tank top and say, "Here, you can have this."

We'd brought in a DJ from Miami who kept the music pumping at full volume all night. "Loud" doesn't quite capture the experience. The music was so deafening that there really wasn't a way to have a conversation. When kids would step outside for air, they'd talk very loudly because their ears were fried from the sound.

Most of the kids who came to the rave had driven or gotten a ride from a friend. Had parents caught a glimpse, I'm pretty sure not one would have dropped off their child there. (Also a good night for parents not to be too hashtag savvy!)

By the time the last student had passed through the entry turnstile, we'd welcomed nearly two thousand teenagers to the event.

The auditorium, reeking of sweat, was a madhouse. The floor and walls were shaking as over a thousand kids jumped up and down. Some teens were getting jostled around in the crush of the crowd. Kids were getting up on each other's shoulders. Some were crowd surfing. Others were getting kicked in the face by crowd surfers.

One student paused to tweet, "Covered in sweat that's probably not mine."

Honestly, it was a little gross.

Throughout the evening, my team and I scrambled to manage the event while putting out fires. The coat checkers needed more change. The security guards turned over confiscated alcohol. Someone's car got dinged in the parking lot. Someone needed a bandage. Someone else wondered if we had any diet caffeine-free soda. I wish caffeine had been our biggest beverage concern.

Clearly, the eight security guards we hired weren't enough to keep a lid on the madness.

Throughout the night I found myself half hoping the adults would show up and take care of all the messes. Then I realized, *We're the adults!*

Between mini-emergencies, we were glued to our phones, monitoring the #orphanrave hashtag. Wanting to preserve the integrity of what we were about, we were furiously untagging many of the posts.

Foul language? Untag.

Drinking in the hallway? Untag.

Shorts too short? Untag.

It was pretty stressful.

When the music finally ended, just after midnight, and the lights came back on, I felt a wave of relief wash over me. If I'd been able to hear, I'm sure I would have heard a big sigh as I exhaled. As kids flooded out of the building and back to their cars in the parking lot, I breathed a quiet prayer that everyone would drive well and get home safely.

When we'd paid all the bills, we'd made more than $26,000.

And that is how we built our first home in Uganda!

GOD'S ONGOING LEADING

Ever since God had laid the word *orphans* on my heart, I'd been actively researching what the church and other nonprofit organizations were doing to support orphans, in hope of creating a nonprofit that could make a real difference in the lives of those God loves. I'd spend hours surfing the Internet to learn about those who were doing the most effective work around the globe. The more I researched, the more I discovered that a majority of leading nonprofit organizations were not making the level of impact they could with the finances that had been given to them, contributing as little as 20 percent of donations to the actual cause. This did not sit well with me.

Utilizing many of the same skills and resources I'd used to launch the store and host events—building, organizing, promoting, selling—I continued to work toward meeting the needs of vulnerable children.

BE WHERE YOU ARE

Some of the books I'd read over the previous year, featuring heroines who left the only lives they'd ever known to move to India, Cambodia, or Uganda to change lives, reminded me that traveling overseas to help others doesn't have to be the path for everyone. I didn't sense that it was mine. Having given me a heart to care for orphans, God was asking me to be faithful to Him, equipping His church, by using the resources I had right where I was at.

If you're still a student, or if you lack the funds to travel abroad, please know that you don't need a stamp in your passport to make a difference in the world. Maybe you encourage your parents to provide respite foster care for a child who's been orphaned in your own community. Or maybe you volunteer at the Boys & Girls Club in your city. God might call you to teach Sunday school to eight-year-olds and share about His love for them and for a world in need. Whatever God has called you to do, it will begin *right where you are.*

Maybe even in a Starbucks.

CHAPTER 10

EVERY YES MATTERS

God uses our yes to bring life out of death.

If I'm honest, I expected moving day for eight Guatemalan orphans to be a lot better than it was.

Let me fill you in. Hope of Life had been started by a Guatemalan man named Carlos Vargas. Carlos grew up in extreme poverty but made it to the United States, where he became a successful businessman. Married with children, Carlos became wealthy, but something was still missing in his life.

Carlos explains, "I spent twenty years in the United States, thinking about me. Just me. Every dollar I made was for me and my family. All I had was money. There was no way God was going to get to me."

If you know anything about God, those are dangerous words. And, as is God's way, God did capture Carlos's heart.

Carlos became ill, bedridden with several diseases, including gout. After four and a half months in bed, unable to walk or use his hands, Carlos told his wife that he wanted to return to Guatemala to die. Back in his homeland, a homeless man who was also blind came to visit Carlos and prayed over him. Carlos began bargaining with God. "God, forgive me. I am so poor. . .all I have is money. Give me another chance. Get me out of this bed and I will dedicate my life to the poor."

He prayed that prayer many times, and within a week Carlos was miraculously healed.

Carlos knew he'd made a business deal with God, and he was prepared to honor his end of the contract. With a new commitment that his inheritance would not be money but would instead be a legacy, which is a treasure in God's eyes, he began helping the poor and needy people who came to him for help. Then he bought three thousand acres of land. If you were flying by in your private jet, at first glance the scenic property, nestled in the lush mountains of Llano Verde, might look like an exotic resort. But a visitor wandering the property would soon discover that those who live there and are served there are not the wealthy. In 1987 the ministry began by meeting the needs of elderly people who were homeless, abused, and abandoned. Two years later, a little boy named Andres who wasn't being cared for by his family was brought to live on the property. Since then, the campus has become home to a school, a hospital, the elderly home, orphan homes, and more. Truly, it's like the Disneyland of God's love on earth. In addition to saving children like Andres, today the ministry trains church planters, distributes aid, implements clean water projects, cares for orphans and children with disabilities, and builds homes, schools, churches, and community centers.

Carlos proudly runs the ministry like a business. For example, a school he established that serves 500 students welcomes 250 who are able to pay for their education, and 250 more, like the orphans who live on the property, who are not. Smart, right? I was wildly impressed by Carlos's savvy as a businessperson who used his gifts not to make a buck for himself, but for the sake of God's kingdom. Those gifts equipped him to multiply the work that was happening on the ground. Personally, since we shared some of the same gifts, I found it very rewarding to see Carlos in action.

Though Carlos had escaped poverty, many in Guatemala do not. During my visits to Hope of Life, I'd leave the ministry compound to spend time with the children living in filth at the city dump. Shoeless, with cuts on their feet, they'd step through glass while searching through garbage looking for a meal. Sadly, they'd become accustomed to the horrible smells of the country's sewage system, which made me feel nauseated.

The bleakness of their situation was heartbreaking. That terrible scene was actually one of the reasons I quickly became enamored with Hope of Life's mission. The heartbeat of the organization—whether through education or evangelism or child rescue—is saving lives. Hope of Life rescues children like Andres who aren't getting the care they need in their homes or like those living at the city dump.

Before the orphan homes were built at the foot of the mountain, children were housed temporarily in a large facility at the property's crest. Rescued from death's grip, they began to experience the security of daily food and a place to lay their heads. They began to trust. They began to grow.

When I sat down for lunch with Carlos Vargas in Zacapa, Guatemala, on a shaded patio outside the ministry's office center, I began to hear his heart for orphan care. As he shared his vision for a different type of orphan care, my heart quickened. What he was describing was exactly how I'd imagined doing orphan care, in family-style homes. If I was going to be involved in orphan care,

I wanted it to be done right. Carlos already had several American couples lined up to move to Guatemala. God had spoken to these families, and they were just praying and waiting for God to speak to others to build the homes for them to live in.

That would be us.

DIAMONDS AND BOW TIES

To raise the money to care for more children, friends and I hosted a black-tie gala event at Tulsa's luxurious Mayo Hotel. Businesses sponsored tables, bringing their own guests, and we also hosted a silent auction. Individuals purchased tickets for $100 each. The amazing and inspiring Bob Goff, author of the *New York Times* bestselling book *Love Does*, was our speaker, and his vivacious energy animated the room.

Two things happened that evening. For starters, we raised $60,000 to build two homes on the campus of Hope of Life International. And secondly, lots of people wearing diamonds and bow ties were offered a taste of life that really is life. As Bob spoke, I prayed that as children living in poverty were being knit into families, people with plenty would be willing to use their wealth to live out the good purposes God had for their lives as well.

PRAYER LOG

At the lunch with Carlos, he'd said something that lodged in my mind.

He'd declared, "When you're working with God and raising money, His abundance is greater than any earthly wealth. Instead of asking people to give, ask the Lord!"

Those words really challenged me, because I'm a doer.

If I say I'm going to do something, I will. I'll make it happen. I'll work diligently to complete the task, and my natural tendency is to focus on my own resources and abilities. Unfortunately, this can-do mind-set had prevented me from recognizing God's overflowing abundance.

After leaving lunch that day, I began to write down my prayers to the Lord in my prayer log and track the ways God was answering them. Today it's exciting to look back and see His answers and timing.

GRAND OPENING

Gentry joined me on a trip to celebrate the home's opening, and her fiancé, Kevin, came as well to serve as our videographer. The day before, we joined others who were scrambling to make final preparations before the big dedication party. We prepared the beds for children who'd never had a permanent home of their own. Those of us working to get the homes ready were full of anticipation. To us, knowing the children would be moving in the next day, it felt like Christmas Eve.

But the next day, when I saw the children making the journey down the mountain, carrying their belongings in a plastic bag or a tattered suitcase a mission group had left behind, I began to have concerns. Their faces, uncertain about a future they couldn't predict, looked more like what you'd expect to see after the Grinch stole Christmas. Kids who'd already endured such seismic ruptures in their lives—some who'd lived with siblings at the dump, one family who'd seen their father kill their mother, others rescued from abusive situations—looked sad and confused as they trudged down toward the newly built homes. Having never experienced a stable permanent living situation, they only knew that they were being uprooted once again. Though their large group home had been only a temporary solution, the staff there were the only caring adults some of them had ever known. Now they were being asked to endure yet another uncertain transition.

Had we done the right thing? Had we made a mistake in building the orphan homes? Would it be an institutional Band-Aid that wasn't meeting children's deepest needs? I prayed it would not, and from what I learned from all my research about best practices in caring for orphans, I believed in what we'd built.

These homes had been conceived and designed with care. A couple of loving parents would anchor a home-like setting with ten children. Each home had a kitchen and living area, as well as three bedrooms. The parents had one, and there was a room for girls and a room for boys, each of which had three bunk beds. There was also a bathroom off the hallway, a true luxury in impoverished communities. There were three homes like this on campus, and all of them would include children of both genders so that siblings would never have to be split up in different homes.

If the couple serving as house parents already had children of their own, those children would, of course, also live in the home. There wouldn't be shift workers who'd return to their own families when the workday was done. There wasn't an industrial dining complex like on college campuses. Biological siblings weren't separated by age for convenience; they were always kept together. The orphan homes had, in every way, been built to knit children into a loving family where they could be protected, nurtured, and loved with God's love.

When the children who'd looked so nervous walking the half mile down the mountain prepared to enter their new homes, though, I could see they were feeling anxious but also excited about whatever was next. We all stood outside together for the dedication, singing, praying, and committing the homes to God.

HOMECOMING

After the dedication, the children were released to enter the houses. The older ones ran inside. I followed one little girl, who was four, inside as she searched for the bed with her name, Paula. When she found it, her round brown eyes widened. She reached out hesitantly to touch the pink flowered comforter.

Sandra, one of the house parents, smiled and said, *"Mira quien esta por encima de ti. . ."*

Look who's above you.

Glancing up, she saw her older sister, Sophia, stretched out on the bunk above hers, grinning at her.

Paula, continuing to stand in awe, flashed a huge smile. Sandra coached, *"Es tuyo. Usted puede establecer en él!"*
It's yours. You can lie down on it!

Hesitant, as if the bed might break, Paula lay down and placed her head on the satin-soft pink pillow.

I wandered throughout the homes, watching children marvel at beds and sinks and toilets and chairs.

During the dedication, Carlos had prayed that the children living in the new homes would know the love that their heavenly Father had for them. The next day, when we flew back to Tulsa, I continued to beg God to make it so.

LISA AND JASON

During this season, I met a couple in Tulsa who also had ties to Guatemala. Jason was in the oil business, and his wife, Lisa, homeschooled their three girls.

When Lisa and Jason had gone to Guatemala on a short-term mission trip, they recognized the way that the country's educational system limited children from developing the full potential God had given each one. Primary education, from about the ages of seven to fourteen, is free and obligatory. But because the schools, many located in remote rural areas, are poorly funded, many lack access to textbooks and the curriculum they need to become educated, which would help break the poverty cycle. There are many private schools in the country, but the majority of the rural poor are receiving a second-rate education that ends before high school.

Convinced that education could open new doors of opportunity for children, and even change the nation, Lisa and Jason returned from their trip inspired to make a difference. The couple used their own personal funds to translate, print, and purchase books for public schools throughout the country. When God opened their eyes to a need they could meet creatively, Lisa and Jason said yes.

When we allow God's Spirit to open our eyes to a world in need, our open hearts are softened to the things that move God's heart. A lot of people who have gone on short-term mission trips, like Lisa and Jason, return home, seal their hearts back up, and continue on with the lives they were living. But when we do that, our hearts harden. And the next time the Spirit tugs, we're less likely to notice and respond. I'm convinced that

Lisa and Jason's first yes, to a short-term mission trip, opened their hearts for the next yes. And mobilizing their resources to provide needed educational materials for children kept their hearts soft for the next need. When the next need comes their way, the couple is already in the habit of seeing what God sees and saying yes to Him. First, time. Then financial resources and rich networks. And eventually, their hearts and home.

Lisa and Jason are living the kind of adventure Bob Goff had invited generous, well-heeled Tulsans into. They are living life that is making a difference for the kingdom.

FAMILY LOVE

When I returned to Hope of Life nine months later, I was dying to know how the children who'd moved into our homes had adjusted. Let me just tell you, these little ones were more joyful than any American kid I've ever met.

What had been birthed in those nine months was more than I could have hoped for.

After I arrived, I dropped my bags off at the guesthouse and wandered over to one of the orphan homes. I sat on a bench near the home, shaded by a silk cotton tree, watching the kids play. What I witnessed exceeded even my biggest prayers for these precious ones.

Children were running around outside, playing ball and jumping rope. I knew children were resilient and, even in the most desperate environments, adjusted to their circumstances. What I hadn't anticipated was something that wasn't measurable, the way that personal toothbrushes or three meals a day might be. What I saw in them was *security*. Remembering past trips I'd taken, I half expected the children to rush over and climb me like a jungle gym. But these children kept playing their games as I watched them. And I noticed that whenever they'd have a need—a question to ask or a skinned knee—they no longer swallowed their pain because there was no one who cared. Instead, they'd run inside to seek comfort from one of the house parents. Orphans no more, they trusted their cares to a mother. And a father.

These children who'd come from such dysfunctional and constantly changing situations were thriving with the consistency of a loving family where moms walked their kids to school, siblings worked on homework to-gether, and families shared meals.

That afternoon I was invited into the newest home—really, because the children were so visibly transformed, it was hard to call it an "orphan" home anymore!—to share dinner with the family. While I sat nearby, I watched the children wash their hands, set the table, pour water into cups, and, adding one extra setting for their American guest, place the napkins and silverware at the table. After we all gathered and prayed over the meal, they offered me first dibs on a large, family-style bowl of chicken and rice. Though I didn't understand all of the Spanish during the meal, I watched as the kids made jokes and laughed together, as a mom asked a child with a lot of energy to settle down, and as a dad encouraged a quiet child to speak. Simple interactions I would have taken for granted in my own home had been made *beautiful* by what God had done for these children.

After dinner the children helped to clear the table and wash the dishes. Then we gathered together for evening devotions. The father in the home read a scripture passage and shared about what it meant for his family. We sang worship songs while some of the children banged on tambourines and shook little maracas. After devotions, the kids washed their faces, brushed their teeth, pulled on their pajamas, and climbed into bed.

As I sat in the living room, I could hear the busy whispered chattering coming from the girls' room. I glanced at a workbook belonging to one of the young boys that was sitting on a shelf in front of me. A boy named Santiago had written his name on the cover. Santiago had lived his entire life with crippling cerebral palsy. Before Hope of Life, he'd had extremely limited mobility and even less hope for a good future, as families in his country often disown children with disabilities. As I thumbed through the pages of his workbook, I saw that Santiago had colored beautiful pictures of his new home, his new parents, and his new siblings. The one that gripped my heart was a picture he'd drawn of himself riding his scooter in the courtyard alongside the other children who were playing. No longer an outcast, he belonged to a loving and nurturing family.

YES

God's love being poured out on children didn't happen in a miraculous or magical way. It happened because a number of people who loved God said yes to the prompting He put on their hearts. God can do great things with our small yeses.

Carlos Vargas said yes to serving the poor in Jesus' name. The house parents said yes to leaving the country of their birth because children, not yet their own, needed parents. People in Tulsa said yes to an evening gala. Others said yes to writing additional checks. I said my own yeses, which eventually depended on others'!

Jesus' feeding of the five thousand, recorded in the sixth chapter of John's Gospel, depended on a little boy who was willing to share his lunch: some bread and some fish (John 6:1–14). Sit with that for a minute. In the first century Jesus chose to use the meager resources offered by a little boy, and He still chooses to use whatever we're willing to offer today. As we unclutch our grip—on our money, our time, our energies, our addictions—God can do amazing things with our crumbs of bread and stinky fish.

In the face of hunger, Jesus filled bellies. And Jesus continues to replace want with abundance and bring life out of death. When Carlos Vargas faced death, he was revived and an entire life-giving community was birthed through him. Orphans struggling to survive were placed in families. The beautiful pattern of God's redemption is that He brings life out of death.

As you search for your calling, as you tip your ear to the sound of God's voice, you can expect that God will bring life out of death. Maybe, like me, you will find that the loss of the life you've dreamed of will drive you deeper into God's heart. Or maybe, as with Carlos, a physical challenge you're facing will deepen your relationship with Christ. As you face disappointments, as your dream is disrupted, notice the ways God is near, and listen for His gentle voice.

I don't know what your yes will look like, but I'm convinced that God is waiting for it. For most of us, the yes isn't going to mean resettling in another country. (And even when it does, there are a lot of other yeses that precede that one!) Right now, God is inviting you to lend your yes to growing His kingdom. Maybe that will mean volunteering to tutor kids after school. Maybe it will mean channeling part of your clothing budget to feed, clothe, or house children in need. Maybe it will mean agreeing to befriend a teen who's struggling or a single mom who is working long hours to care for her children. The kingdom runs on hearts the Spirit has softened to say yes.

God will use your yes.

CHAPTER 11

OUT OF EXCUSES

*God asks us to sacrifice both our
comfort and our resistance.*

Going to another country with a random guy my friend
Layna met on Twitter sounds like a sketchy proposition,
right?

Yeah, I thought so, too.

Layna had connected with David Nelson after he'd
tweeted about a contest to win a trip to Haiti. She
tweeted back, entered the contest, won it, and ended
up learning more about David and his ministry in Haiti.

Layna, whom I had just met, knew that I was passionate about orphan care. During our time together scrolling through pictures of my recent trip to Guatemala,
I'd shown her photos of the special needs children I'd
been working with. One picture of a tiny baby, dressed
in a royal-blue and orange Florida Gator onesie, sparked
the idea in Layna's mind that her friend David, former
wide receiver for the Florida Gators team, and I should
connect regarding our similar organizations.

But my life was full. The yogurt shop was busy, caring for children had me traveling the world, and I had no
interest in going to Haiti. I was pretty open to wherever
God would lead me, but Haiti was the *one country* I'd
sworn I'd never return to. My family and I had been in
Haiti for a day as the last stop on my Make-a-Wish cruise,
just one day before my seizure in Taco Bueno. As we
were eating and shopping in parts of the city cultivated

for tourism, I felt uneasy in my spirit, and the market had felt dangerous. And though it didn't occur to us at the time, we later learned that voodoo practices and witch-craft rituals were prevalent there. As we learned more about the spiritual warfare on Haitian soil, a few months after our trip, my mom even felt convicted to get rid of everything we'd purchased there—a response to what she believed God was asking her to do.

You know that meal that you once ate before getting seriously sick? And the disgust that comes to mind at the mere thought of attempting to eat the same food again? That was Haiti to me.

When I'd begun my journey helping orphans, I'd made it very clear: *I won't go to Haiti.* There were plenty of children in other countries who needed help. The team I worked with agreed.

Doing a friend a favor on his way home from prac-tice, David left me a message on my phone.

And when I gave him the courtesy return call, David followed up and we chatted on the phone and shared our stories.

David had grown up in Texas and was playing football for the New York Jets. He admitted that he first visited Haiti as a publicity op, but he fell in love with the children there. He shared his story of meeting one young boy who had been living on the streets. When David gave him a protein bar, he didn't want it. Instead, he held up his arms to be held. That boy changed David's life. So David began a ministry to help children in Haiti, where he lived in the off-season. David and his brothers believe in equip-ping Haitians, through discipleship, to find their own solutions to the poverty they face, and his organization,

I'm Me, is doing just that. Haitian staff run the ministry, and he spreads the message, grows the ministry, and invites donors to support it.

I shared with David a bit about what I was involved with in Uganda, Guatemala, and our newest boys' rescue home under construction in Brazil. I think we hung up feeling like we had both honored Layna's wishes.

After all, I'd already made up my mind about Haiti. *There. Was. No. Way.*

Whenever people would ask me why I wasn't interested in engaging in ministry in Haiti, I spouted a standard reply: "I don't feel like the Lord's calling me there." If I'd been completely honest, though, I would have confessed, "I despise that place. I really do. And part of me associates it with my cancer relapse. I want nothing to do with it. I'm sure God loves Haiti, but God will send someone else who is passionate about it there—like David!"

A few days after our phone call, David e-mailed me to encourage me to join him on a trip to Haiti the following week.

I politely declined, expressing how much fun it sounded, but I was just too busy. I'd been studying human trafficking and was overcautious of everything with any degree of safety risk. The whole scenario of going to a foreign country with people I had never met was just too close to the stories of the girls I was studying. After all, our only connection was my friend whom I'd just met, who'd met him on Twitter. I wanted to work toward solutions for vulnerable children, women, and girls around the globe, not *become* one.

"I'm actually going to be in Tulsa Wednesday night.

I'm flying home from New York to Dallas," he replied, "and if you want to grab a few friends and meet for dinner, that would be great. If not, no pressure."

He was pretty clear in his heart and mind that the Lord was telling him I needed to go to Haiti.

And I was running out of reasons why I couldn't go.

I BLAME LAYNA

I felt like it was all Layna's fault.

Layna and I had met through Racheal, my small-town sorority sister. Racheal and Layna had been friends since they were little. As Racheal recognized that my passions from the days of our sorority world had been shifting to helping fight injustice in the larger world, she insisted I had to meet Layna, certain we'd hit it off.

"Y'all are just alike," she promised.

She wasn't entirely wrong.

Layna, whose biological father is a Saudi Arabian prince, was raised in the United States by a single mom whose life was changed by Christ when Layna was young. Layna has an amazing heart for people. Right out of college, she moved to Russia for two years and served as a missionary. She has gone to Greece with Christine Caine's A21 Campaign, which fights against human trafficking, spending six months in a rescue home there for trafficked women. God has given her a passionate heart for people of Middle Eastern descent, and she prays faithfully for the Gospel to break out there. It's her dream. And yes, she is a princess.

I'm more and more convinced that God is looking for other young women like Layna who are more committed to growing God's kingdom on earth than they are to building their own kingdoms.

Wednesday night, friends joined David and me for dinner at a classic American restaurant in downtown Tulsa.

David described the work he and his brothers were doing in Haiti, raising up the next generation of leaders by caring for the children. Layna had been right that we were both passionate about caring for children who were precious to God's heart, but I already knew that Haiti wasn't for me. There were plenty of other places to serve, but it was clear from David's countenance that he was enlivened when talking about the country.

As the evening ended, I politely promised David that I would pray about whether the Lord was calling me to go to Haiti. Yet I also reminded him how busy I was.

In that moment, I had no intention of going home and praying about it.

But, my word being my word, and with Layna's encouragement, I did go home and pray about it. If you haven't learned this yet, praying can be dangerous. Not spewing out words at God. There's no risk of hearing from God if you never stop talking. The dangerous move is to listen. And that night, my heart softened by God's Spirit, I listened.

I heard God telling me that I should go to Haiti. "Really, God? . . . No!"

Over the months I'd spent listening to God, it had become very clear that God was calling me to serve the orphaned children He loves. But I thought that meant Uganda, Guatemala, Brazil, and every other country but Haiti.

But God was showing me that although we may have one thing in mind, God may have something entirely different in store for us.

I've seen it time and time again in the lives of women who are purposing to be faithful to God. A woman who would love to be married offers her singleness to God and He multiplies that time by birthing new passions in her heart. Another woman, bent on climbing the corporate ladder, is drawn by God into marriage, motherhood, and ministry! The temptation, for me anyway, is to hang on tightly to my own plans. We can get tunnel vision about what we want and close our eyes and ears to the Lord's leading.

What I was discovering, though, is that releasing my fear—trusting that God's plan would be better than my plan—would shine a light on the path before me.

And nine days after the courtesy phone call, Layna and I were landing in Port-au-Prince.

RELUCTANT TRAVELER

There were six people in our group that week: Layna and me, David and his brother Patrick, who worked on the ground in Haiti, and two men who'd mentored them. The two men, probably in their early forties, reminded me of my dad and were really personable. But there was no doubt, Layna and I had ended up on a bro trip!

David's organization, I'm Me, had a house in Port-au-Prince that hosted groups interested in learning how to impact the lives of children in Haiti. David and Patrick took us all over the region to expose us to as much of the country, the people, and the ministries as possible.

During our stay, we visited a Saturday feeding program. I noticed Franschesca the moment we walked in. She was about four or five years old, wearing only an oversized pink T-shirt. Shoeless, her feet were covered in cuts, like those of so many children living in poverty. Her skin was ashy and her hair was matted and knotted. Her large black eyes were pleading. When I gave her a smile, she came over and sat in my lap.

Franschesca's body felt warmer than June in Haiti should feel. When I lifted the back of my hand to feel her forehead, the way my mom would do when I was sick as a girl, she was burning up with a fever.

While the other children were running around having fun, playing with a red rubber ball David had brought for them, Franschesca remained in my lap, wilting.

The afternoon of our second day, Patrick and David took us to one of the most dangerous areas in Port-au-Prince. They really wanted to show it to their mentors and gave Layna and me the opportunity to bow out. Willing and even eager to witness the realities faced by children in Haiti, we chose to go. Patrick, David, and five Haitian men took us to a rough neighborhood that Americans were discouraged from visiting. Wanting to make sure Layna and I were safe, David had two Haitian bodyguards assigned to me, and two to Layna!

As we walked between rickety shacks, stepping over trash and raw sewage, hordes of children followed us. Some of the smallest ones were naked. Others wore only underpants. The little ones begged to hold our hands and walk with us. The weight of the poverty and the spiritual brokenness felt very heavy, and as we'd expected, the area didn't seem safe at all. Layna and I could feel men staring at us. Soon after, our Haitian protectors felt it, too. Aware of the danger, they hustled us into the van we'd arrived in and got us out of the area.

Over the next few days, singing with the children, playing at the feeding program, and learning more about the culture, I began to understand why David was lit up for the country and why he'd wanted us to go.

When my mom picked up Layna and me at the airport after our trip to Haiti, I recognized visible relief on her face. While my suitcase was lighter on my return trip from Haiti, my heart came back a little heavier.

During the season I'd spent in quiet prayer listening to the Lord, God had given me a love for orphans. I had a huge heart for Africa, but I felt as though now God was opening my eyes to the need much closer to home. It was mind-boggling to realize that in Haiti I was just seven hundred miles from the beautiful resorts I love to vacation at in Florida.

My fear of and resistance to Haiti simply couldn't hold up against God's great love for the people who lived there.

That doesn't mean that Haiti wasn't as dark as I remembered it to be. It actually was. The witchcraft and voodoo beliefs felt as heavy and deathly as the suffocating poverty. But I was more aware than I'd ever been that just as Jesus had come to shine as light in the world's darkness (John 1), He also identified His followers, you and me, as the light of the world (Matthew 5:14).

Haiti, so close to home, was a place of desperation in critical need of the love of God to shine brightly.

As you open yourself up to receiving and obeying God's plan for your life—the plan for you that's better than you can imagine and better than you can orchestrate—your yes will most likely require sacrifice. Sacrifice isn't very popular these days! It's not a virtue retailers are paying to advertise on Facebook. But the way of Jesus is the way into which I was being invited.

God was inviting me to sacrifice the plans I'd made to keep building in Uganda.

To sacrifice pursuing a successful career to pursue the work of ministry.

To sacrifice a more typical dating life to wait for the husband He had for me.

To sacrifice fear.

Comfort.

Privilege.

DAVID'S GUESTS

I'd done some bookkeeping at the yogurt shop on a Tuesday evening and stopped at a Whole Foods grocery store on my way home. I was wandering through the aisles with my list when I saw a little girl about the age of Franschesca, holding on to the side of her mom's grocery cart. It dawned on me in that instant that I never followed her home. Did Franschesca even have a home?

The Lord continued to prompt my heart with one word: rescue.

Twenty-four hours later, I'd purchased my ticket.

The Lord had taught me to spend time in prayer the week before these trips. Specifically, I always pray for supernatural intervention in regard to those He wants to put in my path. I pray, "Lord, if there is any child You want me to rescue, send them my way!"

Upon landing in Port-au-Prince on a mission to find little Franschesca, I was greeted at the airport by Patrick, a girl named Lauren, who was I'm Me's newest in-country team member, and Chantelle, a dancer for the Dallas

Mavericks. David was flying in later that afternoon.

The next morning, we all drove the jeep to the village by the feeding program, about forty-five minutes outside the city. When we started showing Franschesca's picture around, we were sent down a long alley. Franschesca's "home" was a light grayish-blue tarp draped around wooden stakes. We learned that Franschesca lived with her father, mother, and a few siblings. Our translator explained to her father who we were and that I cared about Franschesca. Though she was still quiet, she looked much more animated than she had when I'd seen her previously. Her father was kind and gentle, and it was obvious she was well loved.

When we arrived back at the house after finding the sweet girl on my heart, I was trying to reason why God had called me back to Haiti on a rescue mission. Then, David received a phone call. He looked deeply interested in what he was hearing.

"Mmm-hmm. . .yes, that's them. . .okay. And can you give me that address one more time? All right, *mèsi*." Haitian Creole for "thank you" sounded very much like the French *merci*.

"Witza and Georgina were left at an orphanage. I'm not even sure how they knew to call us, but I'm going to go visit them."

David's home had cared for Witza and Georgina until a relative had abruptly removed them from care. David and his team hadn't been able to track them down.

When we located the orphanage, we parked in the street and went inside. What we saw and smelled made my stomach churn. Several toddlers ran around in thin T-shirts, wearing no diaper or underwear. Infants were lying in their own waste. The stench on the hot June day was overpowering. All of the children we saw were thin. Several, appearing dehydrated, looked pale and lifeless.

When we finally spotted a teenage girl, David asked our translator to ask her who was in charge. The girl, quiet, looking a bit fearful, disappeared and came back several minutes later with a woman who appeared to be in her forties. She looked suspicious.

"*Ki sa ou vle?*" she demanded, asking us what we wanted. Her hair was held back with a green bandanna, and she wore a dress and sneakers. She looked well fed. Her arms were crossed in front of her chest, her knees locked in a defensive posture.

David coached Matthew, "Ask her if Witza and Georgina are here."

Dutifully, our translator inquired, "*Nou ap cheche pou de ti fi ki te rele Witza ak Georgina. . .*"

Though I couldn't understand the woman's response to him, I did recognize belligerence when I saw it. I heard it in her tone. She wouldn't look at anyone in our group, and her eyes even darted away from our translator.

The teenage girl who'd fetched her disappeared further back into the building.

David continued to press, challenging the owner about the conditions the children were living in. Government orphanages were funded according to how many children they could claim, and he knew that corrupt managers often pocketed monies intended for child care. His tone became more heated as the conversation continued.

As they talked, I sat on the floor playing with one child. The little girl, wearing only a pair of shorts, seemed to be around three years old. Her hair was rigid from malnutrition. She would move only slightly, but would stare deep into my eyes. I was trying to get her to warm up to me, but she was so weak. As we played, I kept one ear on the conversation between David and the director of the orphanage.

While they argued, the teenager reappeared and Witza and Georgina were with her! They ran to hug Patrick and David.

As David continued to reprimand the woman, she became visibly upset. Then he threatened to contact the government and have her facility shut down.

When she stomped off, David and Patrick conferred together.

Turning to our small team, David announced, "We can't leave all these kids here. We're going to take Georgina and Witza home, and we're going to take as many of the others as we can get in the van with us. So we'll start with the ones who look the weakest and youngest."

At that point, everything began to happen very quickly. The woman reappeared and began to yell at Georgina and Witza as they moved toward our van. Our translator spoke firmly to her and instructed the girls to keep moving.

The rest of us each scooped up a child and carried them to the van. I grabbed the little girl whom I had already been playing with.

I kept my eye on the director of the facility. She seemed upset, but perhaps afraid of being turned in, she did not protest the removal.

Before we left, David explained, "We're going to get these kids healthy and then bring them back." Then his tone shifted from anger to a pleading desperation. "Please, take care of the others."

EXODUS

The hot, crowded van smelled foul as we held the smallest children on our laps and bounced over rocky streets. Our translator told us that most of the kids had never ridden in a car or van, so the older ones, though weak, were delighted by the ride. We asked him to explain to the children who could understand what was happening. His face flooded with kindness as he explained to them that we wanted to feed them and help them feel better.

We were quite the crew as we piled out of the van back at the house: five Americans in our twenties, who'd never been parents, suddenly had nine children to care for!

Patrick beelined for one of the mamas who lived on the property to help. Bursting through the front door, she threw her arms around the disoriented girls. Surveying the room, she seemed to understand what a big job she had before her and immediately began pulling out tubs and rags for bathing.

Then Patrick asked one of the other young women, Lauren, to help him take the two babies to the doctor. They scooped up both frail infants, who looked like skeletons. The mamas and I all helped to wash each of the remaining seven children. Georgina and Witza seemed to know how to bathe, but the other five—as if they'd never had a bath—simply allowed us to wash them. As we gently ran a cloth over their skin, I saw each one visibly relax, as if they knew they were safe. After bath time, each of us offered our clean T-shirts for the kids to wear as knee-length gowns. After they were clean and dressed, one by one the girls sat on a kitchen chair as the mamas gently untangled and braided their hair.

David had gone to the store for food and bottles and diapers for the babies, but we knew we needed to be careful about how much the children ate, as their systems were so weak.

After they finished grooming the children, the mamas began fixing an evening meal while the rest of us entertained the children with the simple toys and books that were in the house. We knew that the move could feel traumatic, and we wanted to be as gentle as possible with them.

Pulling every chair and stool in the house to the table, we wiggled together to accommodate everyone. One of the mamas held the two infants to her chest while the other served small portions of rice and chicken to the eager older children.

One little boy, named Wilson, was about five. Though the children quickly devoured the food on their plates, he saw that some of the rest of us still had food on our plates, and began pointing and crying, saying he wanted it. He also pointed at the food in the serving bowl, whimpering. It was so wonderful to watch the Haitian mamas speak to him. I could tell they were reassuring him that he would be fed again the next day.

CULTURE SHOCK

I flew home from Haiti on Friday so I could attend Steph's baby shower on Saturday morning. On the car ride from Tulsa to Oklahoma City, I thought of the children at David's house.

Putting on earrings and a necklace for Steph's party, I could see how much God had changed in my life. He'd gently demolished the barriers I was aware of, like my fierce resistance to having anything to do with Haiti. And he'd even exchanged my dreams, for a comfortable life with a husband and children, with His dream for *all* children to know His love and provision. God knew I still desired to have my own family one day, but as that dream became bound to God's dream, I knew it would also include continuing to care for more of the children God loved.

As I stepped out of the car and headed into the party, I was catapulted from Port-au-Prince to the baby shower that Stephanie's sister-in-law was throwing for her, and the shock was mind-bending. She received designer baby outfits, a designer diaper bag, and a high-end baby stroller! Because I knew many of the young women and family members in that room, I knew they were excited and only wanted to bless Steph and her new baby. The contrast, though, between the poverty of the dozens of children we'd seen in the orphanage and the luxuries that one child would enjoy was hard to process.

More than anything, what I saw was a mom who was thrilled to welcome her child into a world in which she could provide for her. Still holding those nine fragile children in my heart, I thought of their mothers. Some, perhaps, had died. But I also knew that desperate Haitian mothers who were unable to feed their children would vie to place their children in orphanages where they had a better chance at survival. And, apparently, even some where they might not.

I loved celebrating with Steph the new life coming into the world. But when I drove back to Tulsa later that afternoon, my mind continued to wrestle with the discrepancy. Between snippets of conversation with my friends, my mind scrolled through all the children I had met around the world. I begged God for answers: *Teach me, God, how to best love the children You love.*

A few years earlier I never would have believed that my heart and mind and spirit would be fixed on the children in Haiti. My heart had been set on the life that everyone else was living, and I couldn't picture any other. But when I'd offered God my broken heart, He'd infused it with His life.

His heart.

His passions.

His plans.

In that process of researching and studying further ways to care for more children through a nonprofit organization, I discovered that developing nations, like Haiti, Uganda, and Guatemala don't need another nonprofit! In fact, many of these countries were already limping along with the help of countless nonprofit organizations. And though most Christian organizations were feeding the hungry, people were still in desperate spiritual need. In many cases people had been exposed to Jesus but hadn't been impacted by Him in a transforming way. Convinced that the local church was called by Jesus to be the hope of the world, I began to dream about how I might use what God had given me to strengthen the local church. In that process, God led me to launch an organization to rescue the unreached and underprivileged children around the world. The With All My Heart Foundation would exist to ensure that 100 percent of every donation from public giving would go toward helping those in need.

Unlike other nonprofit organizations, the With All My Heart Foundation would operate as a nonprofit, providing resources and meeting needs of the community, but the people living in the countries we serve wouldn't know our name. Instead, they would only know the name of the church. That way they would see that the body of Christ was meeting their deepest needs—it was Jesus who fed them, clothed them, cared for them, and loved them.

CHAPTER 12

BONDYE NOU AU GRAN

God is passionate about saving souls through the Gospel.

"Bondye nou au gran. . ."

I woke to the sound of a Haitian child singing outside the room where I'd fallen asleep under a mosquito net–covered bunk bed. This time, though, David wasn't the one hosting first-time visitors to Haiti. . .I was!

Eight of us had made this trip to see the work in Haiti. Jeff Ragan was the founder of Kize Concepts, and he'd brought three guys from his leadership team; my sister and brother had come; and also a friend of ours. After landing in Port-au-Prince, we drove three hours to Lascahobas, just a few miles from the border of the Dominican Republic. Like much of Haiti, the home, surrounded by protective walls, gates, and guard dogs, was located in a dangerous area where riots were common. Arriving after dark, we'd been ushered to our bedrooms and sent straight to bed.

". . .chante avèk mwen, Bondye gran. . ."

The singsong voice belonged to a girl who sounded as if she was three or four years old. *". . .Tout moun kapab wè. . ."*

Eyes closed, I could feel sunlight penetrating the thin curtain of the sparse bedroom, flooding in around the bare frame. As when refusing to wake from a sweet dream, I willed my eyes to stay shut.

". . .Koman Bonye gran."

And though the little girl was singing in Creole, I knew every word. The song by Chris Tomlin, "How Great Is Our God," was one already knit into the depths of my heart.

The same way the Spirit often breathes fresh life and meaning into scripture when it's read in a new context, the words of this song were being animated for me in a dynamic new way as they danced off the little girl's lips. When my mom had sung it with Gentry and Bradley and me during morning devotions when we were very young, I knew the words were true. When she and my dad hummed it beside my bedside at St. Jude's Children's Hospital, the words buzzed again with a fresh veracity. And now, as I heard the words from the lips of an orphaned Haitian girl, the truth about God's faithfulness that I'd experienced for myself exploded with new meaning.

The vulnerable little girl continued to sing, and in the syllables that would have been meaningless if spoken without the familiar melody, I heard the words that had encouraged my own heart in my most vulnerable moments. As I slowly opened my eyes, peering out the window for a glimpse of the angel who'd serenaded me awake, I mused that the day probably couldn't get any better.

I was wrong.

FABIE'S MINISTRY

Wearing a floral romper and flip-flops, I left my room to look for my friend and hostess, Fabie.

Fabie, a thirty-eight-year-old Haitian woman, had grown up in one of Haiti's more privileged families. Five years prior, she'd been working as a nurse in Port-au-Prince when she began to pray, asking God about His purposes for her life. She was a practicing nurse at the hospital during the 2010 earthquake and experienced the traumatic aftermath of all the children being displaced. As an answer to one of those prayers, a family friend gave her a plot of land in Lascahobas, Haiti. Two years earlier she'd opened a home for orphans as God had directed her to do.

Across the hall, I found Fabie preparing breakfast for our team. As Fabie cooked the eggs over an open fire, I asked her about the little girl whose song had begun my day so beautifully.

Fabie, who'd also heard the singing, told me that the girl's name was Esther. She'd been rescued by Fabie as an infant and raised by her ever since. Found by villagers wearing only a dirty ripped shirt, without a diaper, Esther had been left in the outdoor kitchen area of someone's hut. One of the neighbors had alerted Fabie, who'd come to rescue the helpless infant.

The name Fabie had chosen for this sweet baby seemed particularly fitting for my young songstress. Esther in the Old Testament became a queen when she wed King Ahasuerus. But the Jewish girl who'd been raised in exile in Persia by her cousin Mordecai had been an orphan. Then, when she became queen, she stepped out in faith and was responsible for saving the life of Mordecai and the Jewish people. Queen Esther saved her nation.

My heart was captured by Esther's joy. While I didn't want to romanticize the faith of this girl with very real physical and emotional needs, I did recognize in Esther—and also in Fabie—a deep joy that many well-fed and well-resourced women I knew in America hungered for.

Though I would have said in a heartbeat that God meets the deep needs of His children's hearts, I recognized that timeless truth in a fresh way through precious Esther.

So it seemed altogether fitting that a vulnerable orphan, placed in a new family who was teaching her the ways of God, trumpeting songs of God's greatness, would be named Esther.

KIZE

Two weeks after driving home from Edmond, Oklahoma, for Steph's baby shower, I found myself driving right back to Edmond to be the speaker for Sam Bradford's golf tournament benefiting St. Jude's.

I'd spent the previous few weeks processing what the Lord was revealing to me about Haiti, and knowing that my board and I had mutually agreed never to go to Haiti, the chances of convincing them that this was the Lord's leading were slim to none. So, sensing the Lord's leading there, I wrote the possibility in my prayer log and continued to pray over it.

At the Oak Tree Country Club I shared my story at the front end of the tournament, before the golfers were sent out to play. I shared with them how I used to be a St. Jude's patient, and now I was helping children around the world, the same way St. Jude's had invested in children like me.

After hearing my heart for the world and Jesus, Sam, who'd organized the tournament, introduced me to a friend of his who had a huge heart for international missions and was looking for a way for his business to make a global impact for others. Jeff Ragan started Kize Concepts, a protein bar and healthy living company. Now, he was sensing it was time to use his business to make a lasting impact and encourage his team of employees to do so as well.

Eight months later, Jeff and the Kize team joined me in Haiti.

GOLMON

One day on our trip, the team decided to venture out and meet families living in the community.

We had a fifty-pound suitcase full of bags of rice and beans. We had packed it with the intention of delivering food to every hut surrounding Fabie's neighborhood, one by one. However, Fabie had advised us that there was one man in the neighborhood who was struggling more than the rest. His name was Reginal Golmon.

We started down the dirt path leading to where we believed Golmon's house was located. Trekking through the village, we were greeted by toddlers running outside, while parents peeked out from huts to view the odd strangers wandering through their neighborhood.

"Golmon?" we'd ask. The men and women would point, and we continued following in that direction.

We knew we had found Golmon when we reached a tarp hung neatly over sticks from a tree. The slim, six-foot Haitian man welcomed us into his home. Our team of nine couldn't all fit inside, so we took turns, rotating in groups of three.

Golmon was caring for three children. His oldest daughter, Catty, helped care for the youngest two. He began sharing his story with us. A year prior to our arrival, Golmon was in a motorcycle accident, resulting in a badly injured leg. The little money he did have was used to admit him into a hospital. He didn't have the finances to fully pay for the surgeries he needed, so he remained crippled. In the midst of his tragedy, Golmon's wife left him and their children. Unable to work, he was struggling to survive. . .unable to care for and feed his children.

The day we arrived at Golmon's home, he had been praying that the Lord would send his family food. His kids were hungry and weak. And the Lord provided fifty pounds of rice and beans, delivered straight to his doorstep. The tears rolled down Golmon's face. Our team had made a new friend.

EYES OPENED

After lunch, we piled into Fabie's white truck and drove to a nearby village, bouncing along bumpy gravel roads. Because there were no roads to the village where we were headed, we parked beside a road and walked about a quarter mile up the side of a small mountain. Chickens and the occasional frail goat wandered in and around straw huts that were perched precariously along the side of the steep hill. We dug our feet in sideways to gain traction, reaching out to use trees for leverage and balance, stepping sideways to ascend the slope. Young children in these huts, who'd never or rarely seen pale Americans, would peek their heads out and holler to one another.

When we'd finally scaled the steep hill, we arrived at a village situated in an open clearing. The lush green trees belied the desperate poverty of the people. The flimsy huts had been constructed from an array of found materials: wood, straw, tin, plastic. They were in much worse condition than the straw huts we'd passed on our climb. Yet, despite the material lack in the community, the children's eyes danced with curiosity and delight at the odd foreigners who'd landed in their village.

As Pastor Emmanuel spoke to a woman holding a baby, introducing our admittedly odd group, curious children and adults began to gather. Most wore clothes that were faded or ripped. One boy who looked to be around six years old wore only dingy gray underpants. A thin mother, who appeared to be in her early forties, had short braids around most of her head and a puff of hair over her forehead. The angles of her bony limbs protruded from a faded gray cotton shirt. The baby on her hip had rust-colored hair, signaling malnutrition.

The children and adults who were gathering eyed the bags of gifts we'd brought: plastic sacks stuffed with T-shirts, tennis shoes, markers, paper, and other items. There were also a few guys carrying machetes, who circled the perimeter of our group, sizing us up. As some began to grab at the items, Fabie instructed us to release the bags, and the people in need descended on them, grabbing what they could get.

Though I had complete confidence in Fabie, that scene really made me nervous. If I read her face correctly, she also seemed a bit concerned. There were just too many factors out of our control. I had trusted God for my own safety before, but now I was asking God to protect this whole team of people for whom I was responsible.

As about forty adults and children gathered around us, Fabie translated for us. "Tell them that we wanted to bring them a gift," I instructed.

Fabie spoke the words in Creole, and when the villagers answered her, she translated for us Americans, "They say thank you."

I continued, "Let them know we're excited to meet them."

She translated, and I saw smiles ripple across the group.

We spent some time talking, through Fabie, learning about each other's lives. We'd been told that witchcraft was rampant in Haiti, and even more so in remote areas like this one. One woman described the demons that plagued her incessantly, even speaking to her during our visit. I could see her get distracted at times, seeming to drift from the conversation as she shifted her attention to the persistent voices.

Though we hadn't gone to the village with an explicitly spiritual agenda, I asked Fabie if we could pray with them, and the villagers agreed. Jeff offered to lead and Fabie translated his prayers, not for God but for our new friends. As we all bowed our heads, we thanked God for them and asked that God would meet their needs. When we heard Jeff conclude with a familiar *amen*, we added our own, but when we heard Fabie's translated Creole *amèn*, our Haitian friends didn't add their own.

After the prayer we continued to chat, via translator, with the villagers, asking them about their lives. As we did, a little thought began to nag at me.

I prompted Fabie, "Ask them if they know Jesus."

She translated my question, but a translator wasn't required to interpret their answer. Dozens of faces simply stared at her blankly.

"Ask them if they know the Son of God, the King of kings, the Lord."

Again, they didn't seem to understand. Blank stares.

Thinking maybe they spoke a different type of Creole that was getting lost in translation between me and Fabie and them, I offered Fabie more prompts.

"Ask them if they know Coca-Cola," I suggested.

She did, and their smiles and nods told me they did know Coke!

Noticing one little boy standing on a deflated soccer ball, I nudged, "Fabie, can you ask if they know Cristiano Ronaldo?" It was a long shot.

She asked if they knew the Portuguese soccer player.

Nodding and smiling, little boys kicked their legs as if they were playing soccer, and the adults nodded, confirming they knew Cristiano Ronaldo.

"Fabie, ask them again if they know Jesus," I requested.

Their faces again negated the need for Fabie to translate their answer.

Suddenly the bags of supplies we'd hauled up the mountain seemed meaningless as God allowed us to discern the greater need of this village: *their souls*.

GOD'S HEART

Though we'd stumbled upon this remote village in the most unlikely way and under the most random circumstances, I have no doubt, to this day, that it was no coincidence.

Even though the souls of the people living in remote villages had not been a priority to me, these precious lives were of highest priority to God. And He was revealing to me that the lives of those He loves who don't yet know Him depend on our generation.

Realizing that Coca-Cola and the World Soccer

League had done a better job reaching the ends of the earth than the body of Christ, I became aware of our generation's negligence in fulfilling our greatest calling—to save a world living in darkness—and it was glaring.

In our neighborhoods, workplaces, and even remote foreign villages, God is inviting us to take the Gospel to those who are dying without it. And not unlike my own dire diagnosis, what's at stake is a matter of life and death.

That's where Jesus' surprising formula for living explodes with traction and meaning. As we lose our lives in small ways and bigger ones—risking social status by sharing the Gospel with a coworker, taking time off work to participate in a mission trip, moving toward someone who makes us feel uncomfortable—death gives way to life.

That's the rhythm of the life that satisfies!

In the first century, no one expected a religious teacher killed on a cross to do anything other than surrender to death. But in the unlikely exchange that marks God's redemptive story to rescue a lost world, death gave way to life—not just for one, but for everyone.

Friends, not only have we been called God's children, but we've been entrusted to carry the Gospel to the ends of the earth—and we've been equipped with every spiritual resource to do it. Life, new life that will be birthed in the hearts of the lost, will spring up as we choose to lose our lives for what matters most.

Some of us take out loans to go to college. Some receive gifts to vacation after graduation. We make monthly payments for our cars. We sign mortgages for homes. We find a way to leverage what we have to get what we want. Can we be as creative in leveraging our resources, even giving them away, for the sake of others? Whether you live near Lascahobas or Tulsa or Los Angeles, and whether you live with little or with plenty, God longs to use you to share Jesus' life-giving message with those in spiritual poverty. And I'm convinced that, as we do, we'll discover the life that truly satisfies.

THE GIFT OF THE GOSPEL

When I asked if anyone in our group wanted to share about Jesus, my friend Omar volunteered.

With Fabie's help, Omar began by asking the people in the crowd what they needed in their lives. Those who were sick asked for healing. Those who were hungry asked for food. Everybody needed something.

Then he proceeded to tell the crowd about Jesus. But the Jesus he described wasn't an American with handouts who'd bring sacks of stuff they needed and wanted. Omar described how the One who had everything made Himself nothing to be among us. Jesus, he explained with love and passion, was the hope of the world.

"He gives you peace," he promised, pausing for Fabie's translation. Passionate, he continued, "He gives you hope and purpose. He heals the brokenhearted and binds up our wounds. He gives you joy in your heart. He's what you need to make it through each day. And He heals all of your sicknesses. All of them."

The more fired up Omar was about sharing the Gospel, the less often he paused to let Fabie translate! Yet when he did let her get a word in, I could see faces flush with lightness and hope.

"Who wants to know Him?" Omar asked. "Who wants

to have their hearts filled today?"

Fabie repeated, *"Ki moun ki vle konnen l? Ki moun ki vle ke yo plen jodi a?"*

"Who wants to know the Savior who created you," he asked, "and live your life for Him?"

As hands started going up, as heads started nodding, I couldn't believe what I was seeing. There was such desperate need, both materially and spiritually, in this community, and they all wanted Jesus. That's all they wanted.

Our mission team prayed again, this time for people to receive Jesus. The youngest one to raise a hand to receive Jesus was probably around seven, and the oldest, in her sixties, was the woman with demons. The scene felt like stories I'd read in Acts where a whole household—in this case an entire village—was saved.

After the prayer we asked if there was anything that people needed healing for. Every hand shot up.

One woman asked for healing for her sick baby.

Another had an injured leg.

Another had been suffering from what seemed like the flu.

We prayed one last time before sliding down the mountain to drive back to the compound.

To my surprise and delight, and I still can't fathom how it was possible, the day Esther woke me up with singing had gotten even better. That—the fervency in my heart after witnessing God's redemptive power for this remote village—was better than any pleasure I could have bought or borrowed. After trekking back down the side of the mountain and returning to Fabie's compound, our team had to head straight to the airport.

The "high" of witnessing what God can do with so little stayed with me as our group returned home, quickening my heart to remember that we serve a mighty God who wants to do miraculous things through us.

AMAZING NEWS

Several days after we returned home from our short visit to Haiti, sitting outside at Starbucks with my laptop, I opened an e-mail from Fabie, who'd received a report from Pastor Emmanuel about the village. The morning after we prayed, he'd reported, those who'd gathered and received salvation woke up to the work of God's miraculous hand spreading throughout the village. Specifically, many of the villagers who'd been sick woke up well. Bodies had been healed just as I'd witnessed hearts being transformed.

I was floored! I knew that God was gracious and wanted to make Himself real to these precious ones who'd put their trust in Him, but I was still blown away by the holy serendipity of God's grace in that village.

And while I was clear that salvation and growth in the faith were God's business, not ours, something didn't sit right with me about sharing the Gospel and then leaving. That seedling of concern was one God would continue to water and nurture.

When I finally fell into my own bed in my house that night, the words Esther had sung to wake me continued to dance in my head. The friends we'd met that day had chosen to trust the name that is above all names. But I knew that God had more, for them and for me.

God has more for you, too.

OUR GENERATION

In every town, neighborhood, and home, God is calling women and men to lose their lives and change the world by reaching every tribe, culture, and language.

Sadly, the urgency of that reality isn't being trumpeted in many of our lives today. Even in the church, we get it upside down and backwards when we exchange Jesus' mandate to lose our lives for the pleasures, the stale substitutes, of this world.

We live in abundance, yet too often we have poverty mentalities, clinging to the worldly pieces of our lives that make us happy, while failing to realize the abundance of the kingdom of God surpasses any earthly gain.

If we're communicating that knowing Christ allows for chasing false substitutes for our hungry hearts, then we've forsaken the One who died and who asks us to die to ourselves. The Gospel that is truly good news for the poor is one that brings life to those who are dying, like Omar did on a Haitian mountainside, and it calls those who live with selfish desires—like me, like you—to give up our lives for the sake of the kingdom of God.

Maybe that will look like trekking to a remote Haitian village, but it could happen in your neighbor's kitchen. It might mean starting a Bible study in your hall at your college dorm. It might mean inviting young kids in your neighborhood to participate at your church. It could mean inviting a coworker out to lunch a few times and sharing the Gospel with them over a nine-dollar salad.

Because God doesn't want any soul to perish (2 Peter 3:9), you and I have been charged to make known the name that is above all names and worthy of our praise. May the mighty name that falls so naturally from the lips of an orphan in the world's poorest nation also be spoken with conviction by you and by me. We are the ones God is calling to make Him known throughout the earth.

WHAT'S NEXT?

The night I received Fabie's e-mail about what God had done in the village, I lay awake marveling at God's goodness. That I'd been privileged to witness God's salvation in the lives of His children seemed almost too good to be true. But part of what kept me awake that night, and so many since then, was the thought of all the villages and communities and people who still hungered for the good news of Jesus. Too many have not heard because those of us who know Him are not going and not sharing.

Three years prior, I'd been focusing only on orphan care, but God continued to show my heart even more needs. One of those pressing needs involved the unreached people who had never heard the Gospel. The new dream the Lord had given me wasn't without obstacles. God used plenty of interruptions in my path to open my eyes. I even faced fierce resistance from people I wouldn't have expected it from, but where the Lord was leading, I knew I had to follow. And His blessing came with it!

The With All My Heart Foundation was growing faster than I had ever dreamed. We were making Christ known around the world, through both physical and spiritual interventions, in the lives of His children.

Not only was my heart for orphans expanding, but God was giving me even bigger dreams. I'd continue to hold those in my heart until God showed me what to do next.

It wasn't anything I'd seen coming.

CHAPTER 13

LIFE INTERRUPTED

God interrupts our plans for the sake of His.

Landing in the country of the world's vastest rain forest, friends and I jumped off a plane to be greeted by a burly, bearded mountain man who towered over the Costa Rican men.

His name was John Hutchins.

"Welcome to Costa Rica," he greeted as he set down the sign holding our name. (The sign really hadn't been necessary.)

We hopped in John's truck to begin our journey. He was an American from Minnesota who had moved to Costa Rica a few years back because, well, God interrupted his plan.

John was rough, he was big, and he was unlike any missionary I'd ever met. We began chatting during the car ride. Instead of selling us on the work of the organization he and his family had started, John told us stories about his adventures within the country. By adventures, I mean running through the country's crocodile banks and spending the night in the rain forest with leopards. Those kinds of stories.

"We'd run on the banks as the water was sinking, and these eyes would creep out of the sand from beneath our feet," he narrated.

Two guys had traveled with my friend and me, and one of them was my brother, Bradley. He and his buddy were on the edge of their seats, soaking in every word John was saying.

My friend in the backseat smiled over at me and asked, "How did you meet this guy?"

I whispered back, "I found his story online."

The guys were eating it up, asking, "Just how close were you to the crocodile?"

We wove our way through Costa Rica's famous coffee fields, which supply Starbucks and many other coffee companies, until we reached our destination, right in the middle of the coffee farms in Atenas.

As we arrived at the home of John and Jill Hutchins, Jill was waiting for us on the porch.

Jill was a fireball! She was motherly but fierce.

Inviting and hospitable, she welcomed, "Grab a seat on the patio. I made us lunch."

She pointed in the direction of a shaded patio.

"Oh," she warned, as if it was an afterthought, "and watch out for tarantulas. They are everywhere around here, especially in rainy season."

As we made our way to the back patio, Madi and Mari, the Hutchinses' two daughters, fed us fruit off all of the trees in their backyard.

"Try this one," Mari coaxed. "It tastes like a weird combination of apple meets flower meets honey."

"Oh, and this one," Madi raved.

We tried just about everything they gave us.

Madi warned, "Look out for the little worms that sometimes crawl into the fruit."

Okay, no more fruit.

We sat down for lunch, and as the family shared, the Hutchinses' story gripped me. All of us lapped up every word they had to say.

John and Jill responded to Jesus' call and were sent

to Costa Rica to be missionaries. While I think it can be tempting to assume that people who are sent into the mission field are "a certain breed," I promise you that John and Jill are nothing like any missionary family you would expect. John had been running a general contracting company, and Jill had been a high school Spanish teacher. That's about as normal as it gets, right? But as they were living their normal lives, raising their two daughters, God called the Hutchins family to Costa Rica to assist in a ministry to poor migrants from Nicaragua who were working in the coffee fields.

Well, they listened. It was uncomfortable and inconvenient, but they listened.

When you spin through the coffeehouse drive-through on the way to work, you're probably not thinking about where the coffee beans, ground to aromatic deliciousness, began their journey to your twelve-ounce paper cup. If your coffee came from Costa Rica, the beans may have been picked by my friends, the Nicaraguan immigrants.

Nicaragua, where a majority of the nation lives on two dollars a day, is the second poorest country in the western hemisphere behind Haiti. Because parents do not have the resources to feed their families, poverty has forced many families to sneak across the border to seek work in Costa Rica.

When they leave home to work in the fields nine out of twelve months a year, these families know they risk being caught and even that there might not be a job waiting for them when they arrive. Parents will carry children on their backs through the rain forests, pursuing the possibility that a job in the fields will help them feed their families. They eagerly want to work and provide basic necessities for their children's survival. They live in any shack they can find. Many families will live together, squeezing over a dozen into flimsy huts built with branches and covered with leaves.

Children over the age of six work the fields with their parents from sunup to sundown, carrying huge baskets of harvested red beans. Many of these fields are on the sides of mountains, where it's difficult, carrying nothing, to stand without falling.

Without grandparents or other community members to care for their young children, parents are forced to leave children younger than six in an open area all day, praying that no ill befalls them. But danger does come. Children have been abducted, abused, bitten by snakes. One baby drowned in the floods following a rain. Desperate parents had no other option than to leave their children alone.

When God called Jill and John Hutchins to Costa Rica to be missionaries, they didn't know what was ahead of them. All they knew to do was to step out in faith. John sold his business. Jill quit her job. They sold their home and moved. It was a decision the whole family made together—even their middle school–aged daughters agreed that they wanted to do something for God with their lives.

Changing the world is never an accident or a coincidence. It's a result of choosing to step out in faith when God begins to speak to you about His plans for your life. John and Jill understood that.

You know how they say the way to a man's heart is through his stomach? Well, the way to a mom's heart is through her child. And serving these families opened the doors wide for the Hutchinses to share God's love with them.

PESCADITOS DEL SALVADOR

Recognizing the desperate need of these parents who lacked the financial resources to keep their children safe, John and Jill started watching the children of a few Nicaraguan families during the day. Before they knew it, word spread throughout the coffee farms, and more and more families began to leave their children to be watched. Even though John and Jill were strangers to these families, they were safer than the dangers they were up against, and parents learned to trust them. With all the children they were watching, they started running a makeshift child-care service in the back of their home. John, using his contracting skills, fixed up the building, and the girls helped their mom care for the little ones.

When the children would arrive at the child-care center at sunrise, they would be hungry, filthy, and coughing from the environment they were sleeping in. But as soon as these babies were dropped off into the hands of Jill, Madi, Mari, and their team of Costa Rican women, they would give each child a nice warm bath in a bathtub they'd built into the center, clothe them with one of the clean outfits they had stockpiled in their closet, and feed them. This family showered each child with love all day while their parents were working to get their families on their feet.

The next day, they'd do it all over again. Babies came with dirty diapers that hadn't been changed since the day before; the older kids were dirty and hungry again;

and the Hutchinses just kept loving on these little ones.

In addition to caring for them, the Hutchinses wanted to educate the children so they would be able to go to school one day. Jill and her girls taught the children how to read and introduced basic math skills, hoping to multiply every second they had with the children. And every day, without fail, the kids learned a Bible story and talked about Jesus.

When I visited John and Jill, they were serving twenty-two children in the day-care center they ran out of their home! The only problem was, they were renting their home and were running out of space to care for all of these children. They hoped to buy a property better suited to serve sixty active little ones. Though parents weren't obligated to pay for the care, they were required to serve several hours during the week in exchange for the care of their children. For their time working, they also got to pick out two items from the Hutchinses' stash of clothes and necessities that would otherwise be a large expense for the family.

The Hutchinses wanted only to follow God, wherever He might lead. And they were willing to leave behind friends, family, soccer leagues, and summer camps to follow Jesus' call on their lives.

ORPHAN PREVENTION

The way John and Jill cared for the children of those families in need is known as orphan prevention. One of the greatest ways to make sure children do not become orphans is by equipping loving families living in poverty to provide for their own children.

In Costa Rica, human trafficking is prevalent, and

many children who are left in the fields are prone to be trafficked. But providing child care for parents who are willing and wanting to work gives families a much-needed boost. And requiring these parents to help out regularly at the day-care center reinforces the value of the service they are receiving and provides an opportunity for Jill to teach the mamas, one on one, how to better care for their babies.

One of the children, a six-month-old , is one of the babies John and Jill watch every day. She has a headful of fine black hair and full cheeks. Her mother walks ninety minutes a day, up and down the mountain, just to make sure her baby girl lands in the arms of Jill Hutchins.

One evening I had the chance to speak to a few of the parents, asking the mamas how the child-care service impacted their families. As tears ran down one mama's face, she said, "You will never know how much it means to me to know that my baby is safe."

As we look at our lives, whether we're students scrambling to finish term papers or young adults who are trying to fit in yoga, grocery shopping, brunch, and a manicure, it's easy to be consumed by our plans. When I was finishing my last semester of college and running Orange Leaf, I was always paddling to keep my head above water. I get it. Whatever our circumstances, the most natural way to live is to make a plan and then hustle to make it happen.

Finish college? Apply to grad school. Finish grad school? Send out résumés.

Get a job? Start working toward a promotion. Get the promotion? Buy the house.

Own the house? Build the addition.

We feel more secure when we can make plans and then take the steps to accomplish them. We feel like we're in control.

But we were made for so much more. And, graciously, God is in the business of changing our plans. That doesn't mean God is going to force His plan upon your life. God doesn't pick you up like a chess piece and drop you down to live among the unreached people of the Ecuadoran jungle without your consent. God is the consummate gentleman. He knows His plan for you is the best for you, but He wants you to *choose* the best.

Another way to put it is that "no" means "no." If you say no, God doesn't force you into His will.

But if you're willing to open the eyes and ears of your heart, if you're willing to release your fierce grip on the plans you've made, I can assure you that God absolutely delights in revealing His good plan for your life. Think about the earliest believers who encountered Jesus. Their lives were absolutely disrupted. Simon and Andrew, James and John had all planned to be fishermen. Their parents, who were also fishermen, had made the plan when they were toddlers waddling near the shore. But when Jesus said, "Follow Me," they dropped their nets and followed. If they would have chosen to stay and not fully follow, they never would have experienced walking closely with the Messiah at the greatest moment in history.

If you look back in scripture, you'll see that plenty of people *did* refuse to have their plans interrupted! Some said, "Lord, first let me go and bury my father" (Matthew 8:21). When Jesus told a story about guests being invited to feast in the kingdom of God, a master sent his servant to invite the guests. But the guests began to make excuses: "I have just bought a field" (Luke 14:18); "I have just bought five yoke of oxen" (14:19); "I just got married" (14:20). They refused to interrupt their plans to see the glory of God.

We love how God rescues us from the mire of sin, but we're less enthusiastic, less ready to move, when God rescues us from our suffocating comforts. I want you to know, though, that this is how God operates. God might call you through the pages of scripture, and He might call you during *The Bachelor*. God might send a dream to wake you up in the middle of the night, or He might quietly capture your attention during a sermon or worship.

God is an interrupter of plans.

You decide whether or not you will allow the divine interruption to change your life and the lives of others.

A SAFE HOME

On one of our visits to Costa Rica, we visited a home serving young women between the ages of fourteen and eighteen who'd been trafficked. Run by a different ministry organization, the project is tucked away in a private location. Because the girls' lives had been so violated, the program to serve them provided very rigid rights and responsibilities at first, gradually offering more freedoms. Throughout the program, the girls would progress through five small houses.

In the first house, they had very few freedoms or possessions.

In the second house, they might be rewarded with an item of clothing or a Bible.

They received counseling throughout each phase of

the program, and when they responded well, showing signs of growth and healing, they'd move to the next phase. If they showed signs of resistance, like not showing vulnerability during counseling, they would not move forward. Some girls who were deeply traumatized would have trouble discussing what they'd been through. Others were more open and able to share and reflect. Each one reached various milestones at different speeds. The program was tailored so that each could move at her own pace.

They had the most beautiful evening ritual in each of the houses before bedtime. One by one, each young woman would look in the mirror and say, "I am beautiful." The rest of the group would echo, in response, "You are beautiful."

"I am worthy" was met with a chorus of "You are worthy."

"I am loved." *You are loved.*

"The Lord has a plan for my life." *The Lord has a plan for your life.*

The staff of the program invited us to step into each of the empty houses to see how the girls in the program lived. Reflecting their deep respect for the precious lives of those they served, the staff made the experience feel like a very sacred tour.

Reverent, we entered the first home, a simple adobe-style concrete building. This was where girls who'd most recently been rescued stayed. During their time in the first house, girls were invited to contemplate their experience and the conversations they were having in counseling. To eliminate distractions, the interior decor of the home was very minimal. The walls were blank. The furnishings were simple. The young women didn't even have access to pens or paper to write. They were asked to simply focus on their stories and their healing.

When they moved on to the second house, the girls were given a small increase in freedom and received one of their own possessions back, as well as one piece of their own clothing. The interior of the house was still sparse, and there still were no distractions like newspapers or radio or television or games. If they opened themselves to the work of counseling and participated in all aspects of the program, they moved on to the third house.

When we stepped into the third house, I could see the visual difference in the space. The residents of the third home were allowed to make the space more personal and homey. For instance, girls were allowed to hang things on their walls. There were a few prints of landscapes and even the rare photograph of a mother or a sister. I also noticed a few Bibles and other books that were available to them.

When girls graduated to the fourth house, they received another outfit from their personal belongings. This house had colorful walls and reflected more of the personality of the girls who stayed there.

In the fifth home, dressed with curtains and carpets, turquoise chairs and colorful lamp shades, we enjoyed the best part of the tour because we got to meet the young women staying on the property. What struck me most about these teenage girls was how normal they were! I'm not sure what I expected, but they were the kind of girls I'd met before in Spanish-speaking churches. They enjoyed reading, they missed home, and they loved pop music. They were so sweet, approaching us and saying, "Hi, what's your name?" Different features—the bend of a nose or the curve of an eyebrow—reminded me of so many other teenage girls I knew. We could have been visiting a Costa Rican church youth group, and in moments it felt that way. But each time my mind returned to the reason we were meeting, my heart shattered a bit more. I couldn't comprehend the extent of abuse, pain, and suffering that these young girls had experienced. Some of them had been abducted and spent years in brothels; others had been sold between gangs.

When we all grabbed a seat on a chair or couch or on the floor, the staff asked the girls some questions and invited their answers. The questions, about their hopes and dreams, about their families, weren't terribly intrusive. The staff was gentle and kind. And I could hear in the girls' answers a strength and resiliency that signaled God's healing work in their lives. And from the softness of the countenance of some, and from the tone of voice of others, I even suspected I could identify the ones closest to graduating from the program.

Before each one left, her housing and employment and other supports were all in place. Then, when each one was ready, the girls were sent forth one by one, each receiving a festive farewell celebration.

NEW LIFE

As I searched their features—broad faces, black eyes, and coffee skin—I wondered if any of the girls had Nicaraguan parents who'd worked in Costa Rica's coffee fields. Wanting the horrifying reality of human trafficking to be destroyed, I prayerfully imagined how their lives might have been different if they'd been better protected as children.

Seeing John and Jill's day care at full capacity, I left Costa Rica praying that God would send a donor who would contribute to the vision to build an education center to care for the children under age six through John and Jill in Costa Rica. I put it in my prayer log and prayed over it every day for three months, dreaming of how the supports they were offering families could be expanded. Until that day when a generous donor gave me a call—and with the Hutchins family, we began rescuing more kids!

The education center was designed to prevent young Nicaraguan children in Costa Rica from being left alone on the coffee farms by caring for them during the day while their parents work. As the Hutchins family and local Costa Rican staff are able to care for more and more children in need, we are also able to invest in their families, teaching them about Jesus. The center is run by the amazing couple who are now dear friends, John and Jill Hutchins.

THE SACRIFICE

Interruptions come in different ways and in different forms: losing your job, being falsely accused, having what belongs to you taken. When God stops the progress of your own plans, He is often up to something. God may interrupt your life in the form of a tragedy, a broken heart, or a strong conviction that's hard to shake. These interruptions should not be taken lightly. God has a plan that is guaranteed to be better on the other side of the interruption.

When God interrupts our lives with His dream, it can be hard for us to want to step forward to embrace that calling because we see the sacrifice instead of the reward.

That's where faith comes in.

Madi and Mari Hutchins would be the first to tell you that it's not easy moving to Costa Rica in middle school. They had to come to grips with the fact that they would never have a normal high school experience: prom, football games, or friends who spoke their first language. There would forever be barriers between them and everyone else, but that is the sacrifice they made.

These girls traded in their comforts for God's calling. When you ask God to use you, He's going to ask you to do some uncomfortable and inconvenient things. Maybe not as uncomfortable as moving to Costa Rica, but He will put you in situations where you will have to take risks.

World changers are, first and foremost, risk takers!

When God removes comforts from our lives, it's because He has a better option for us. God isn't a taker; He is a giver. God never takes away more than He plans to give back. So as we choose to embrace His calling on our lives, we also need to learn to embrace interruptions.

John and Jill didn't have a dramatic life-and-death experience that gripped their hearts to do more for the Lord and His kingdom. They were just a normal family, longing for something more. They took the Bible seriously, said yes to God, and are being used by Him for the good of others.

INTERRUPTIONS

When the girls we met in Costa Rica were snatched from their families and forced into sexual slavery, the enemy interrupted the plans they had for their lives. But when, by God's grace, they were rescued and delivered to safety, God interrupted Satan's schemes.

God interrupts the power of sin and death to bring renewal and redemption.

When we look at the lives of those teenage girls, we can see clearly that God is in the business of interrupting what's meant for death *for our good*.

It's a lot harder to recognize the goodness of God's holy interruptions when we're satisfied with the treasures of this world. When we *prefer* them.

But just as God's heart longs for girls who have suffered to flourish and to become the women He created them to be, God's heart also longs for you to become the woman *you* were created to be. You were made to live God's plan for your life.

You were made to be a woman who holds her plans lightly.

You were made to be a woman who courageously exchanges her dreams for God's plan.

That's what John and Jill did. It wasn't glamorous. It was inconvenient. There were countless costs to saying yes to God. But when they released their plans, God could use them to fulfill His dreams to eternally impact the people He loves.

And. . .if He hasn't already, God longs to interrupt your dream to accomplish His plan.

Chapter 14

MOTHER OF MANY

God asks us to release our dreams for the sake of His.

"We're having an outdoor concert night for the community," I explained via e-mail. "Do you think you can help me find a band, or singing group, or praise team, to lead praise and worship in your language?"

My girlfriend Natalie had introduced me to a Haitian woman named Yvrose, calling her the most amazing lady she'd ever met. While the description certainly was impressive, I didn't need the most amazing woman in the world.

I just needed a band.

Yvrose responded, "I have the perfect band for you."

UNLIKELY MOTHER

Yvrose grew up in Haiti and escaped the poverty-stricken country by migrating to Charlotte, North Carolina, with her husband, where they attended college, worked, and established a home together. Eager to start a family, Yvrose and her husband conceived, but in her fourth month of pregnancy, she suffered a miscarriage. Three months later, they conceived again, but the second pregnancy also ended in a miscarriage at the end of the first trimester. Certain that God had spoken to her heart, confirming that Yvrose would be a mother to many, they conceived again. And lost another child. Yvrose had conceived and lost twelve children when her husband left her because of their infertility. She was devastated.

Yvrose stayed in North Carolina and continued her job as a third-grade teacher. And she began to have dreams at night in which God showed her a map, which she later learned was of Haiti. She dreamed of a beautiful body of water, surrounded by cliffs made of large stones, but she'd never been to the place she was seeing in her dreams. She had a sense that she was to return to Haiti, but she really did not want to and still had questions about where God was leading her

Then the Lord began speaking even more clearly to Yvrose in prayer, instructing her, "Go back home and serve the people of Haiti."

Those were the last words she wanted to hear. She had escaped the poverty of her home country and now bore the cultural shame of divorce and infertility. Resisting God's call, she remained in North Carolina.

One day, Yvrose received the dreaded phone call that her mother was deathly ill and was given only a few days to live. She flew back to Haiti to honor her mother's last wishes when her mother was miraculously healed. Now, already back in the country, she traveled to the area that the Lord was showing her on the map in her dreams. It was in Fonds Parisien, on the outskirts of Port-au-Prince. Upon arriving there, she was amazed at what she saw: the beautiful body of water surrounded by cliffs that she'd seen in her dream.

NOT MOVING

Yvrose's mother survived, and Yvrose returned to Charlotte.

Toward the end of the school year, a boy in her class accused her of abusing him. She loved her students and was crushed by the false allegation. The case was being reviewed by the school board, and her reputation was damaged. It was a very hurtful and ugly situation.

Yvrose prayed, "Lord, if You bring truth to this situation, I'll return to Haiti." It was the kind of bartering prayer that really gave God a lot of leverage.

The next day, the boy confessed that he'd lied, fabricating the whole story. He confirmed that Yvrose had never abused him but that his mother had coached him to accuse her.

Can you hear echoes of another story? Certainly mine, as someone who was reluctant to return to Haiti! But more significantly, Carlos Vargas had also fled the poverty of his youth and flourished in the United States. He'd never intended to go back, and when he reluctantly returned home to Guatemala, on what he believed to be his deathbed, his life was transformed. God took what appeared to be a dead shell of a life and planted it in the rich Guatemalan soil where it sprouted, blossomed, and flourished beyond all imagination.

LIFE OUT OF DEATH

In Carlos's story, and in Yvrose's calling, I recognize rhythms of a pattern God uses to liberate and redeem broken lives and bring life out of death: God interrupts our plans for a comfortable life and calls us to fulfill His dream of growing the kingdom.

When Moses, a Hebrew by birth, was raised as an Egyptian in the house of Pharaoh, he had access to wealth and power and prestige. But when Moses saw a Hebrew slave being abused, his eyes were opened to the suffering of his people. In what can only be described as a radical act of downward humility, God called Moses to deliver the Israelites out of slavery and into the land God had promised. It was one of those assignments that no prince wants to get, but Moses said yes.

Mary, the mother of Jesus, also got one of those awful assignments most would avoid. She was young, a teenager, and on the brink of marrying a good man, when an angel appeared to her. So far, so good. The angel Gabriel even led by telling her not only that the Lord was with her, but that the Lord *favored* her (Luke 1:28). It was what any first-century Jewish girl wanted to hear. After that, though, Gabriel's announcement became decidedly more difficult: she would become pregnant and give birth to a son, who would be God's own Son (Luke 1:31–32). Though Gabriel promised that this Son would sit on the throne of His ancestor David— which is just about as good as you can get—I suspect the future promise was overshadowed by the present reality. Walking through her village with a swollen belly, Mary would be humiliated. Gossiped about. And Joseph would be, too. After one very reasonable question—"How will this be, since I am a virgin?"—Mary answered God's calling. With a heart that longed to please God, Mary humbly offered, "I am the Lord's servant. May your word to me be fulfilled" (Luke 1:34, 38).

Because we have access to the full stories of these heroes of the faith, we know that Moses led God's people out of slavery and through the wilderness to the destiny God had promised. We know that Mary gave birth to the One who would liberate all of humanity. But on the front end, their callings could have felt like curses. Moses, who lost the only family he had, was demoted from prince to shepherd. Mary exchanged a schoolgirl's dream of marrying a decent man in a celebrated wedding for the shame of being identified by everyone in her village as a scorned sinner.

If Mary's plan for a comfortable life was shattered by her fertility, Yvrose had been devastated by infertility. The stigma for each was one of shame for a life that didn't look like the plan that was valued by their cultures. Yvrose felt broken, ashamed, and despondent. God's call to return to the poverty she had escaped felt like yet another burden.

ΠOT THERE

"Lord," Yvrose had begged, "I'll go anywhere. Just not there."

Of course, I identify with her struggle on that one. I do.

Yvrose believed that God had rescued her from a land of poverty and hardship, and returning to it felt unbearable. Yet in the end, Yvrose's love for God and her willingness to obey trumped her natural—and very understandable—resistance. But when God answered her prayer, Yvrose returned to Haiti.

And that's where her story, like the stories of so many who joyfully or grudgingly respond to God's call, gets really good. I don't mean that it got easy. That's something else altogether, and isn't actually one of God's priorities. When Yvrose returned to the land of her birth, she found hardship, but the blessings of God also awaited her.

She met and married Pierre Richard, a man who loved her whether or not she could bear his children.

Not long after they'd wed, Haiti suffered the devastating earthquake of 2007. Yvrose, who had been at the airport, returning home from Charlotte with a tent that she had bought in the US, was desperately calling her husband, Pierre Richard, who was late to pick her up due to a flat tire. Yvrose and Pierre Richard had plans to be at their favorite lunch spot that had collapsed in the earthquake. The country was thrown into chaos as families desperately searched for loved ones amid the rubble. God had given Yvrose a mother's heart, and in the desperate aftermath, she and Pierre Richard began gathering up children who'd been separated from their families. Within a few days, they were caring for nineteen children.

She and her husband, with what little they had, pitched a tiny tent to house the children on a piece of land that Pierre Richard had purchased years earlier. As they were assembling it, stretching a tarp over a crude frame, she remembered the vision God had given her in the United States. Though she hadn't thought much about the dream since she'd grudgingly returned, she realized they were building the shelter in the exact place God had shown her.

In the days and weeks following the earthquake, Yvrose and her husband were able to reunite seventeen of the children with their families. The remaining two children, whose families had been lost in the quake, became their own.

When a stranger left a newborn baby boy on their doorstep during the night, Yvrose and Pierre welcomed the little boy into their humble home. When someone else in the village brought them a pair of siblings without parents, they welcomed them in. Eventually the couple was caring for thirty-four children who were once orphans. These children weren't "projects" to them. They weren't running an orphanage. They were a family full of love. These children became *their* children. And just as a mother tells the story of her labor and delivery, Yvrose can tell the stories of how each of her children came to her. Today the older children, some who take college courses on weekends, help with the younger ones.

Sometimes curious strangers ask Yvrose whether the brood are her "real" children. She typically answers, with a glimmer in her eye, "They didn't grow in my belly, but they grew in my heart."

As you might imagine, this family has seen some desperate days. It's hard to imagine caring for one child with nothing more than a flimsy tent. But Yvrose and Pierre Richard obeyed the Lord. Each day they would pray for food. Every morning they'd worship together because singing took their minds off their hungry bellies. When food came, they recognized it as God's good provision.

A SURPRISING LOVE FOR HAITI

God had been cultivating my heart and birthing within me a love for the people of Haiti. On the whole, I found the people to be hospitable, warm, hardworking, and enthusiastic. God had first lit a fire in my heart for Africa, Uganda in particular, and now Haiti felt like Africa in my own backyard, and the need was even greater. Haiti is the poorest country in the world, with a poverty rate of a staggering 72 percent of the population.[4]

My passion for Haiti was personal, too. Haiti was a

country I felt had impacted me negatively, so to claim it as the place where God was sending me to build His kingdom, to claim the ground for Him, felt victorious.

A friend had introduced me to Yvrose over e-mail when I'd been looking for a band. I'd organized a mission trip, serving Fabie's community, and at the end of our week of service we'd planned an evangelism event in the middle of a local village where we'd have music and testimonies and then offer an invitation to know Christ.

When Yvrose had e-mailed back to say that she knew of a band, she explained that the band she had in mind was actually a group of her own kids. Months earlier, the Lord had spoken to one of the older ones, prompting him to begin playing the guitar and to practice leading worship singing. The Lord had showed this boy that He'd use them to reach others as they traveled around the country, leading events that invited others into a saving relationship with Christ. And like a loving mother, Yvrose encouraged her son to believe what the Lord was telling him.

So, yeah, she knew a band.

Yvrose and her gospel band lived about three hours from the location of our community event. She brought eleven children with her that day. On the way, they had a flat tire, causing them to arrive late. When they pulled up to our village, they quickly unloaded their gear and, with smiles on their faces and God's love in their hearts, began to lead worship.

I knew that many in the community had come to check out the music out of curiosity. But as I watched little boys tapping their feet and little girls wiggling their hips, I was in awe of what God was doing in the community and of what God had done in Yvrose's life. Though her plans had been completely disrupted, God's dream was coming to life through her. It was as if God had taken her plans, blessed and anointed her, and set her free to live out His dream. And that dream, which gave love to children and life to a mother, was one of the most beautiful things I'd ever seen. She was filling the longings that were once on her heart through obedience to the Lord.

The community event came at the tail end of our mission team serving the people of the village throughout the week. The With All My Heart Foundation had dedicated our new home for twelve boys who were no longer orphans; we'd led a medical clinic, treating the sick in the community; and we'd built a home for a family in need. We had served this community all week, and now we were going to tell them about Jesus.

I'd prayed about the event with others for months. God had given me a vision of the Gospel sweeping through this nation so that women and men and children would come to know and trust Jesus. I'd seen what God could do when we shared the Gospel on a whim and an entire village had been saved. If God could do that, with no preparation on our part, I expected that God would do so much more with our prayerful, thoughtful preparation and the beautiful gifts of Yvrose's children.

Earlier that morning, I prepared my team for our night concert. As we prayed over the land, I expressed to them that God was about to move in a mighty way. I had seen firsthand the power of God sweep through and save the multitudes. My vision was for hundreds to be saved that evening.

The songs the children sang in Haitian Creole were beautiful. Two men on our team spoke. One shared his experience of being healed by God, and another shared the Gospel, inviting those gathered to respond. As he was speaking, I was praying, and I knew that Yvrose, who was translating, was praying, too.

As we both scanned the crowd to see who would respond, one little man, who was about thirty-five years old, raised his hand.

One man.

Because we had poured so much energy and prayer and hope into the evening, the response was not what I was expecting. And although I understood, intellectually, that the work of God's kingdom isn't measured by human standards, I still felt a little disappointed. And I expected that the others on our team, who'd worked so hard to make the evening successful and who'd heard our stories from the previous year, also were feeling let down by the response.

BEDTIME

By the time Yvrose's kids were packing their instruments and speakers back into the white van that had brought them, it was almost eleven o'clock. Glancing at my watch, I realized it was much too late for them to drive safely back home. Though we didn't have space to host all of them, I told Yvrose that I wanted to get a hotel room for all of them.

That did not go over very well.

"No, you cannot," she insisted. "We have come to serve you!"

I heard in her voice and read on her face that she was quite a formidable woman. Well, I was, too.

"Yvrose, I can't let you drive back on these roads this

late at night. It wouldn't be safe."

She continued to protest, "We will sleep outside before I let you buy our hotel rooms! Please take this money and give it to people in greater need than us."

I eventually met her in the middle and found a pastor's house that she could stay at with her children. Even her acceptance, though, was saturated with love for her children who needed rest.

The heart she had to serve people with the little she had was unlike any person I'd ever met.

After we got Yvrose's precious family settled in at a home that could receive them, our team walked back to our own.

As we walked, we tried to discern why the evening hadn't gone as we'd planned. A few of our team members suggested that it felt a little awkward and uncomfortable that we kept asking if there was anyone else who would like to accept Jesus. They had been with us the previous year and felt it was a lot less uncomfortable when we'd stepped out with huge faith and seen a whole village saved. We'd all been so excited to go back home and tell that story.

Should the message have been shared differently? Had it gotten too late? Should we have shared the Gospel message at a different point in the evening? We kicked around a few ideas, trying to domesticate the wild work of the Spirit, but of course we didn't find any answers. Salvation wasn't a math problem that could be solved with a calculator. It would come only through the breath of God's Spirit.

As I walked to my room, I whispered to God, "Lord, I'm a little confused." I had no desire to host an outdoor concert, but God had put it on my heart to do so.

As I lay in bed, though, and quieted my heart, I heard the Lord speak very clearly. "I come for the *one*."

Whenever I believe I am hearing God's voice, I compare what I'm hearing to the message I hear God speaking in scripture. What God spoke that evening sounded exactly like Jesus' parable about one lost sheep and the shepherd who searches high and low until he finds it. When he does, he puts it on his shoulders and goes home rejoicing (Luke 15:1–7).

"I come for the one."

They were the words I imagined God speaking over me when He rescued me from death.

"I come for the one."

The contrast between God's heart and ours was striking: while we'd been despondent, God had been rejoicing. The whole heavens had been rejoicing.

Between the mission team we'd brought on the trip, the men who'd shared so eloquently and faithfully, Fabie's team, and Yvrose's crew, forty-eight of us had been ministering that night.

God whispered to my heart, "I will send the multitudes to rescue the one."

As I pondered God's unlikely economy, I realized that that one man had a calling on his life and could bring multitudes to Christ. I drifted off to sleep that night wondering what God had in store for him.

Sure enough, we later received news that the one man who had received the Lord had been a witch doctor. God transformed his life that evening, and he loves to share the story of Jesus with others.

PLANS AND DREAMS

When I awoke the next morning, Isaiah 55:8–9 was in my mind, as if I'd been dreaming it: " 'For my thoughts are not your thoughts, neither are your ways my ways' declares the LORD. 'As the heavens are higher than the earth, so are my ways higher than your ways and my thoughts than your thoughts.' "

It was as if God was reminding me, "You can dream your dreams, but it is My plan that will be accomplished."

If the plan for Moses' life that his family had imagined had succeeded, the Hebrew people would have continued to suffer in slavery.

If Mary had rejected God's dream in lieu of her own plan, she would have missed the most amazing assignment ever given to a human being!

If Carlos Vargas had abandoned the deal he'd made with God, thousands of people who've come to know Christ and to find relief from loneliness, despair, and suffering would continue to hunger for physical, emotional, and spiritual nourishment.

And if Yvrose had clung selfishly to the plan she'd imagined for her life, refusing to return to Haiti, countless children would not have known God's abundant grace or been nurtured to become the women and men God created them to be.

As I lay in bed marveling at God's handiwork, I was aware that my story wasn't so different from those of others who'd abandoned what they'd once imagined for their lives. I could have stayed in a relationship or started a business that wasn't God's best for me. Had I clung to my plan for my life, though, I never would have known the satisfaction of what God had in store for me. I may have been able to orchestrate a beautiful wedding and make a large salary and probably would be raising several children in my beautiful home, but I would not have known the deep joy and satisfaction and adventure I've experienced by obeying God's invitation to release my own plans to follow Him.

SEEDS OF LIFE

The wild ride of listening for God's leading and responding in obedience is never dull. When God speaks to me, He shares with me a huge vision. It's one that's out of my reach; it's scary; it's impossible without Him. Instead of showing me the next step, God makes me depend on Him for every step along the way.

When I reflect on the lives of the people I've encountered who are making a spiritual impact with their lives, I realize their own plans for their lives were interrupted. Usually the "interruptions" came in the form of trials. And often the trial was big enough for them to stop and realize that they desperately needed God and that He had something more for them.

Your obedience to following the prompting God is putting on your heart isn't even about you. It's about somebody else! When God calls you to do something for Him, He already has someone on the other side of your obedience waiting on your willingness to obey. That's why our disobedience robs others of seeing God's glory displayed in their lives.

For Yvrose, her disobedience would have robbed thirty-four children from having a home, seven hundred from having an education, and a whole community from knowing about Jesus. If she would have stayed in North

Carolina, refusing to heed God's holy interruptions, she would have robbed herself of experiencing God's purpose for her life and robbed others of experiencing His glory.

God delivers us from the darkness of this world so that we can rescue others living in the same darkness. Yvrose was rescued from Haiti so that she could return to rescue others. When following Jesus our Lord, who came to this world on a rescue mission, we must understand that He intends for us to follow His lead and rescue others.

LETTING GO

Today you might be right on track to accomplish every dream you've had for your life. Perhaps your plans for your education, career, marriage, and children are unfolding on the schedule you always imagined. Or maybe the plans you had for your life haven't materialized the way you dreamed they might.

Maybe, like Moses, you fell out of line for the great promotion. Or maybe God has begun to soften your heart for a people who are oppressed, vulnerable, suffering.

Or maybe, like Mary or Yvrose, you've either experienced an unplanned pregnancy or endured heartbreak because you haven't been able to conceive.

Maybe, like so many of God's servants, you haven't experienced the life you'd imagined would be yours.

I hope you can understand that God's dream for your life may bear very little resemblance to the plans for your future that you've held in your heart. If you are willing to release your grip on them, though, God can lead you through what feels like death into the life that He has designed for you.

If you're in a place today where you're grieving the life you once imagined, I get that. I've known that heart-ache, and I've also experienced God's tender care in the midst of it. Trust that God cares deeply about your heart.

And as you glimpse the liberation of slaves, the rescue of starving infants, the care for orphans, the sharing of the Gospel, and even the adventure God is allowing me to experience, I hope you also can begin to imagine that God's dream for your life is better than you can imagine.

GOD'S PLAN WINS

God is an awesome, powerful God who has ignited every star in the sky. He knows the number of grains of sand on the seashore and in the ocean's depths. He has created galaxies we don't yet even know exist. He has sculpted and painted exotic creatures in the sea that we have yet to meet.

But God is also intimate enough that He knows each of His children by name, and He cares about each one of us. God cares about the desires of our hearts. He knows our hurts and our pains, walking with us through them.

Just as God knows you intimately, God also wants to be known by you. And He wants to reveal His good plan for your life. When you know Him, the rest will follow, because His Word promises that when you seek Him, you will find Him.

If God cares about one witch doctor in Haiti—the *one* He came to save—then He cares about you. And just as He has good plans for that faith-filled man, He has good plans for you, too.

CHAPTER 15

WHAT GOD CAN DO

God uses His people to execute His plans.

When Yvrose picked me up at the airport in Port-au-Prince, she was driving the same white van I'd last seen her driving away from the concert in Lascahobas eight months earlier. We'd stayed in contact and begun to conspire about what we might accomplish together. The With All My Heart Foundation had already started a feeding program alongside her ministry that was nourishing 700 children a day.

When Yvrose hopped out of the van to hug me, I embraced a woman who was living a vibrant life of meaning and purpose. As we bumped along rough roads on the way to her home, we chatted like old friends who were eager to catch up on each other's lives.

HOME SWEET HOME

On the drive, Yvrose excitedly shared with me the story of how her family, of three dozen people, received their home. Though she'd been caring for them all under the covering of a tent, it had been blown away during Hurricane Matthew. Devastated, like so many others in Haiti, Yvrose and her children could only turn to the Lord in prayer. One day they'd been on their knees, praying for God's blessing and provision, when a pale man approached their makeshift camp. The man, a missionary from America, offered to build her family a home using sheet metal. The style looks almost like an aluminum-sided warehouse.

He built one that her whole family squeezed into. Eventually, he built more. In time, two of the homes were joined by an expansive wooden porch with a roof. The home allowed Yvrose to care for her family as she continued to care for those in the community.

When we pulled up to Yvrose's beautiful property, the one God had shown her when she lived in Charlotte, North Carolina, I was able to see for myself the gorgeous lakefront view. It was breathtaking. And I was also able to see the cluster of buildings that now provided safe shelter for her large family.

As I walked into her home, I was greeted by two busy little ones. Jabeta, four years old, was a spunky little girl wearing a lime-green dress. JP, a sweet three-year-old boy, flashed a gorgeous smile that showed off his gleaming white teeth.

Without me even asking for a tour, the kids began showing me around the property that was gradually being developed. Yvrose tagged along.

In a hallway of the main house, Yvrose paused at an open door.

"This is my bedroom," she shared, leading me into a room with a double bed that had a wooden frame.

"What a beautiful bed you have," I said, admiring the nice bed frame.

"Thank you," she replied. "God gave it to me."

I was curious to hear more.

"We had just a mattress, but last month when I was in the village, I met a lady who lost her house in the hurricane," Yvrose offered. Then, as if it was the most obvious response in the world, she explained, "So I gave her our only mattress."

Her story reminded me of the story in Luke's Gospel

about the small gift of the woman who had little that was actually worth more, in the kingdom economy of Jesus, than the gifts of the wealthy.

Yvrose continued, "The next month, a mission team came and asked why I didn't have a bed. When I explained, they bought me a beautiful new bed with a bed frame."

While a bed like that would have been easy to come by at a retail store in Charlotte, North Carolina, I knew it was quite the luxury in Haiti.

JP and Jabeta continued to walk us proudly through the family's property. As we continued our tour, Yvrose paused at her school. In addition to caring for her thirty-four children, she also operated a school that was providing an education for over seven hundred children.

Adjacent to the school was a storehouse where she kept the food she was providing to the students at the school in conjunction with the With All My Heart feeding program. After meeting so many children who were dying of malnutrition, we'd partnered with Yvrose to provide daily meals for these little ones.

We stepped inside the storehouse and saw boxes and boxes of food stacked from the floor to the ceiling.

"We feed seven hundred kids with this food every day. One day the Lord told us to give away our own family's food supply to feed the children in the school. Since that day, we never run out," she bragged. "I just keep giving more away, and the Lord keeps giving more."

So many of Yvrose's experiences with God sounded like stories from the Bible. And, as usual, by God's good design, there was, against all reason, *enough*.

We passed the hundreds of kids who were in class at

school, peeking in their classrooms that were situated beside an open field of land that Yvrose had just acquired. She showed me where they'd build a library for the kids at school, a guest home for missionaries, and homes for other families in need.

"Do you have people working with you to build these projects?"

"Not yet," she admitted. "We are asking the Lord to provide. And when we ask, He answers!"

My faith couldn't help but be bolstered in the presence of this mighty woman of God. Yvrose would often make a powerful statement about God's tested faithfulness that shot straight to your heart. Then she'd follow it up with a smile, like whatever had just rolled off her lips was a normal thing to say. And for her, it was.

I could only muse, *Who is this lady?*

Eight months earlier, the day she turned down my request to get a hotel room for her children and told us to give the money to those "in greater need," I'd assumed Yvrose had a huge facility full of resources. I'd been shocked to pull up to her home and see that her thirty-four children were living in five small sheet-metal buildings.

Yet when she'd proudly described the way God had provided these homes for her, she glowed with a beauty that pulsed with God's light.

Receiving miracles from God seemed to be the anthem of her daily living. When Hurricane Matthew hit and everyone was running to find shelter, Yvrose brought all of her children into a large room and told them to sing praises to the Lord until she returned. Instead of running to find shelter, though, she ran into the torrential downpour to rescue others who were in need.

"I told them to sing," she explained to me. "What else could we do but praise the God who was going to save us from the storm?"

What else, indeed.

This is also the lady who received a five-thousand-dollar donation designated for building a nice bedroom on the property that could be a respite for the busy couple. But because she'd met a family in the village with a greater need, on the day she received the gift, she built a shelter for that family with the money she was to have spent on herself.

"I cannot build a nice place for myself when families sleep under trees," she protested.

The rarity of Yvrose is that although she lives in poverty, she has an abundance mentality.

Her abundance and her resources come from the Lord, and the more she gives away, the more she receives from the Lord.

"If I hold my resources to myself," she continued, "I am only robbing myself of the blessings that God so badly wants to give me. So I just keep giving more and more away and He keeps giving even more to me."

Her description stood in such stark contrast to the mentality of so many of us who live with abundance. We've been taught to save and invest. Sure, we'll give a bit here and a bit there, but never until it hurts. Never extravagantly. Never abundantly.

So how are we to convince a world that we serve a God of abundance when we don't believe it ourselves?

Someone like my friend Yvrose turns the tables upside down, blurring the once obvious line between who is poor and who is rich. The more time I spent with her, the less clear that divide became to me.

AUDIENCE OF ONE

Christine Caine, Beth Moore, and Joyce Meyer all pack out stadiums, sell books, and speak mightily from the pulpit. These women are known around the world, in Christian circles, for the work they do.

Though you might not have heard of Yvrose until today, please add her name to this list of mighty Christian women. She might not be known by many, but she is known to the Lord. She is on the front line every day, taking scripture seriously and living as it says. God speaks to her. God uses her. God multiplies her resources. God hears her prayers and answers them. Though she lives for many, God is the only one she is truly living for, and He is abundant in her life.

Before you put her on a pedestal, Yvrose will be the first to tell you, "I do what I do because Jesus did what He did."

When you truly know Christ, there is only one response, and that is to make Him known.

Today, we live in a world where everybody wants to make their name known, wants to be noticed by others. In a world with so many clamoring voices, we allow the approval and opinions of others to define who we are and who we are becoming. Without realizing the cost it has on our lives, we have become more consumed by the approval of our followers than the approval of our Leader. The dangerous result of glorifying our own name is that the name of Jesus is being glorified less and less. On the other hand, Jesus loves to make Himself known through those who dedicate their lives to following His lead. When we choose to live for an audience of One, our Leader over everyone else, we are choosing to lift up His name over our name.

If you don't have the desire to make Jesus known right now, that's okay. I get that. I still remember that season when I was starting college and couldn't fathom why my friend Lauren wanted to go to Africa to be a missionary. The whole notion seemed absurd and foreign. If that's you today, I want to encourage you to know Him more. I am confident that when you truly know Him, your desire for others to know Him will grow stronger. You will want to make Him known!

Today, as you begin living for an audience of One, you will start to see others in a new light.

PRAYER AND POWER

Prayerful women are the most powerful women because they understand the importance of going before the Lord with their needs. They spend time every day letting the Lord speak to them. Listening to His voice, how He wants to use them. . . As I think about the kind of woman I want to be in three months, or in three decades, the words of Yvrose echo in my ears: "When I pray, He answers."

On the third day of my visit, Yvrose took me to the dedication of a marketplace a few miles from her home. She had been invited by the president of Haiti to participate in the dedication ceremony.

"I don't know why he would invite me," she confessed, "but we should go."

When we finally found a place to park, we joined

the crowd that had gathered. As someone who once deemed herself a shop-a-holic, I thought the massive marketplace was impressive. The twenty-acre facility included ten pavilion-style buildings, a playground for children, seven restaurants, a bank, a pharmacy, and plenty of shopping options. In fact, almost six hundred vendors were represented at this one-of-a-kind market. The venture created countless jobs to bolster the local economy.

More impressive than the market itself was the story behind it. A Christian Haitian man Yvrose knows was crying out to God about his nation and asking the Lord to provide help to lift his country out of poverty. The man spent countless hours praying, fasting, and pleading with the Lord. He begged, "God, You see the hurt. You see the poverty. You see the pain of this country. I ask You, Lord, to send jobs and provide avenues for those who are suffering to escape their desperate circumstances."

When the man stood up from his prayer, his phone rang. It was a pastor in the US.

The pastor said, "God told me you were praying for something."

"Yes, sir," the Haitian man confirmed. "I have been praying for days."

The pastor replied, "God also told me to do whatever it was that you were praying for."

I said you have to be careful about getting involved with a big God, right?

The pastor did obey God and inspired his church to raise $1 million to answer one man's prayer to a God who listens and a God who speaks to those who listen.

Today the marketplace is one of my favorite lunch spots in Fonds Parisien.

KENSIA'S STORY

Yvrose and Pierre Richard care for thirty-four orphaned children. Not only are they not running an orphanage; they aren't even raising typical children. They are raising the next generation of spiritual giants.

Every morning, their family sings praises to the Lord. The heavenly chorus of voices starts with the first child who awakes. This one begins singing, and as other children awake, they join in. Before you know it, all of the children are singing together in unison before the Lord. In the evening, their bedtime routine mirrors their morning one, as the voices of these precious children sing praises to their King. If you were a fly on the wall of this family's home, listening to the sweet blending of voices in praise, it would be easy to forget the earliest stories of these children and the darkness from which so many were rescued.

Four-year-old Jabeta, who'd greeted me at the door when I arrived, was the feistiest little thing I'd ever met. During evening worship, she wiggled in my lap as we offered our praises to the Father who loves us both. Jabeta's story, like the stories of so many of Yvrose's children, is a difficult one. Though births in Haiti most often take place in the home, with the assistance of a midwife, Jabeta was born in a hospital. Yet just minutes after she was born, her mother tried to kill her by smothering her. Jabeta's mother had gotten pregnant by another man while her husband was out of the country. Her mother left Jabeta at the hospital, after claiming that she wasn't her child. It wasn't clear to hospital officials if the mother wasn't able to care for her or didn't want her. But Jabeta was resilient and she survived. When the mother refused to care for her child, a hospital official called Yvrose, who rushed to the hospital to claim Jabeta as her own.

Today Jabeta is just one of Yvrose's many mighty living legacies.

THE LOCAL CHURCH

When our team had shared the Gospel with the rural Haitian village near Fabie's home, God opened my eyes to the millions who have never heard the Gospel. After I'd returned home, God gave me a vision of a *seed*. It was a bit larger than a mustard seed, and much sweeter. In the vision, I knew that when this seed was planted, the Gospel of Jesus Christ would begin to grow throughout the nation of Haiti. Specifically, that growth would happen as trained pastors planted churches in their own villages.

This vision that God had rooted in my heart almost a year earlier was the reason I'd been so adamant about hosting the night concert in Lascahobas, and had believed that the multitudes would come to know Christ.

In the intervening months, I'd even traveled back to Haiti with David Nelson's crew once more, to meet with the head of a seminary in Port-au-Prince. I was eager to discover how the vision God had given me would unfold as the Gospel spread throughout the country.

Like Yvrose, her brother Jeanathon had also been living in the United States, as a pastor in North Carolina, when God called him back to Haiti to begin building the church there. Like his sister, Jeanathon also resisted. He had two high school–aged daughters whom he wanted to see graduate from high school before he moved back to Haiti. And yet, when the prompting of God continued, he knew he couldn't wait.

I related to that desire to obey God, even when it's inconvenient!

But there's more.

God was speaking to Pastor Jeanathon about moving to Haiti at the very same time God was putting this vision on my own heart. So when I met Pastor Jean, as both of us were being obedient to where the Lord was calling us, our visions collided. Together, we have now planted a church on Yvrose's property that serves one thousand people. During the week, the church building serves as a chapel for the seven hundred students from the school, as well as hosting Bible studies and other events.

From that "seed," we are training fifteen new pastors each year through our seminary program to plant churches in their own villages. Pastor Jean supervises the program. These pastors-in-training come to the church one weekend a month to receive ministry training, biblical teaching, and accountability. They've all grown up in the church, have an education, and have recently planted a church or started a ministry in their village. Our heart is to support, unite, and equip them to spread the good news throughout the nation.

One of these pastors has planted a church on Voodoo Mountain, where witchcraft and voodoo are prevalent and where there is violent resistance to the Gospel of Christ. His own parents were killed on the mountain while trying to share the good news of Christ. After their death, he fled the area, but he has returned to claim what was taken from him for God's glory. If this vision to equip pastors to plant churches had been our plan, Voodoo Mountain would be the last place we would plan to go. But because this big dream belongs to a big God, we have every confidence that God's protection is greater than any darkness.

THROUGH HIS PEOPLE

My experiences in Guatemala and Costa Rica, Uganda and Haiti, have convinced me of one thing: God is a God of power who works through His people.

God parted the seas and led His people to safety.

He shut the mouths of lions, and He opened the mouths of whales.

He healed the sick and fed the hungry.

He elevated the unlikely.

He rescued the lost, and He set prisoners free.

Today God is raising up a generation of faithful followers, like Yvrose and Pierre Richard, like Jeanathon and the man who prayed for his community's prosperity. And God is even raising up women like me and like you, who will say yes to God's plan.

Had Yvrose clung to her dream, what would be different about her life today? And what would be different about Haiti?

What about you? What is your dream? . . . How tightly are you hanging on to your plans over the Lord's?

The truth is that God desires to ignite His power in even greater ways through His people today. And that starts with you and me. . .living His plan for our lives.

Chapter 16

EMBRACING YOUR PURPOSE

God has a good plan for you.

As I look back on my own journey—through childhood cancer, and college, and business ownership, and orphan care—I never could have imagined that God would allow me the privilege of being used by Him to change the world. But it has been an equally rewarding privilege to witness others, unafraid to participate in God's plan, releasing their own dreams in order to embrace God's plan.

Writing a book was never a dream of mine. I am not an eloquent speaker, and the idea of putting my thoughts into words makes me cringe. But the Lord kept whispering in my ear, *"Start writing."*

I'd think, *No, thank You. I'd far rather spend my time rescuing children around the world.* But having learned a bit on this journey, I finally agreed: *Yes, Lord.*

Once again, God continued to speak to me. But this time He wasn't speaking about a business endeavor, orphans, the church, or the hungry. This time He was speaking to me about someone else on His heart—*you,* His daughter.

Trying to carefully interpret the message He'd placed on my heart for you, I asked, "Lord, what do you want me to tell her?"

Gently, God said, *"Tell her how much I love her."*

"God," I protested, "she's probably a Christian. I think she knows how much You love her."

And then He spoke these words that gripped my

heart: *"If she knew how much I loved her, she would know the price I paid on the cross, and the greatness of the calling I have for her life."*

Taken aback by His response, I couldn't stop thinking about you, on the other side of these pages. You have probably been through more than anyone knows, keeping much of it inside. You've probably endured brokenness, maybe questioning God for answers to your hurts, and chasing dreams that don't lead to the life you've always dreamed of.

Dear girl, there is nothing I want more than to first hug you, listen to you, and then grab you by the shoulders and shake you up a bit. I'd look you in the eyes and tell you these words:

"You are the most powerful threat the world has ever seen. It's time for you to believe that!"

What if all of Christ's daughters released our dreams, our stories, and our ambitions into God's hands? What if our generation of comparison became the generation of unity and together we traded in meaningless living for the fulfilling life we are promised? What if we were to make Christ known in the darkest places of the earth? Do you understand the impact we could make?

I also see the Lord gently shaking your shoulders and saying to you, "My daughter, your time is now."

YOUNG WOMEN LIKE YOU

I am seeing so many women, just like you, respond to God's call to serve right where they are.

Once a week Candice visits the Tulsa Dream Center, an after-school program for less fortunate children. She drives to North Tulsa to spend time with the kids, and

She teaches a cooking class. Every three months or so she'll have a special event, like going out for pizza or to a baseball game. One year Candice rented a room to host a festive Christmas party for the kids. Though Candice's involvement in these kids' lives began as a volunteer role, the children and their families have grown to trust her. For Candice, investing in these children isn't something she checks off her to-do list. Rather, she's living out God's dream right where she lives.

Hannah Harrell was a spunky little six-year-old with a thick Southern drawl who I met while living at the Ronald McDonald House in Memphis during my time receiving treatment at St. Jude's. Precious Hannah, the oldest sister of two, had been fighting cancer for three years when we met. As her condition worsened, St. Jude's sent her home to spend time with her family. During her last days on this earth, Hannah chose to spend her time hosting a lemonade stand in her front yard to raise money to benefit other sick children who were being treated at St. Jude's. She looked past the darkness in her own life to fight for others.

Anna Taylor, a friend of mine, has a heart for the widows of Kenya. While a student at the University of Arkansas, Anna Taylor founded the James127 Foundation with the vision to use her creative abilities to eradicate poverty among women in Nairobi, Kenya. Anna first moved to Kenya with her family and spent several years in the Nairobi slums helping widows and orphans. Three years later, a Kenyan leader in the slums introduced Anna to a skilled unemployed seamstress, Judith. With an understanding of the slum culture and with widows like Judith in mind, Anna saw beyond the poverty and set out to establish a permanent solution. She graduated from the University of Arkansas with a major in Apparel Studies. Along with the James127 Foundation, Anna founded Judith & James, a high-end fashion line produced for a sophisticated audience dedicated to alleviating poverty and infusing hope in third-world communities.

Brooklynne, a young friend of mine who was a Miss Teen Oklahoma, has a heart for girls in her generation. From her experience in pageants and in modeling, she met a lot of girls who were really hurting. Some wrestled with body image issues or eating disorders, others battled depression, and some had attempted suicide. In the face of so much darkness, Brooklynne is passionate about inviting girls into the light. And she recognizes the way these personal issues can distract us from God's heart for the poor, the hungry, the trafficked, the vulnerable. Brooklynne recently hosted our first With All Her Heart conference, for girls between seventeen and twenty-four, in Tulsa to help women thrive. For this one-day event, we brought in speakers who are working for God's kingdom; they spoke to the girls about their worth, their identities, and the callings God has for their lives. Over one hundred girls heard God's truth about who they are and who they're made to be. God's work in their hearts was a powerful testimony of His desire for all His daughters to be free from the bondages of the world.

I want to provide a place where girls can engage, where they can be strengthened by community and by God's Word, and find resources on how to chase the plan God has for their lives. With All Her Heart is a community of women around the country who are committing to go deeper with God as they discover and live out His purpose for them. We've developed resources and curriculum on how to start your own business or nonprofit. Throughout the week, we provide ways for girls to study and respond to scripture, and once a month girls connect either in homes or online.

YOU

Through this adventure of learning how to trust God, I've begun to recognize some of the twists on the path and also a few of God's ways that direct us to His plan.

1. Release Your Dream

In some ways, embracing God's dream for your life is like swinging on the monkey bars. Before I learned how to master them, I'd balk when it came to releasing my back hand to grab the next bar! Stagnant, I'd hang and eventually drop to the ground.

Grabbing the next bar, reaching for God's plan for your life, requires you to release your dreams. When my plans for my future didn't unfold as I planned, I could have clung to them and resisted God's dream (the equivalent of hanging motionless from the monkey bars). I could have invested my time binge-watching Netflix shows. I could have launched a new business. I could have insisted on my plan.

But I knew that through letting go, God was inviting me to release my dream and reach for His plan. It was that scary feeling of swinging from just one hand and trusting that God's plan would unfold before me. Graciously, it did. But I never would have experienced the goodness of the adventure I've enjoyed with God if I'd clung to the future I once imagined.

My girl, God can be trusted. I know how scary it is to let go of all you've dreamed for your life. But I promise you, it's worth it. When you let go of what's behind you, I promise that God is reliably before you.

2. Expect Resistance

The enemy wants you to stay numb to distract you from the purpose God is calling you to fulfill. And he has a host of tricky moves that he knows you and I are tempted to fall for.

The deceiver persuades you that your dreams—for comfort, for security, for happiness—are more important than God's good plan for your life and for the world.

The deceiver encourages you to compare yourself to others, especially when they show only the shiniest parts of their lives.

The deceiver will use toxic relationships to steal your focus.

The deceiver will use financial struggles—or financial success!—to distract you from God's purpose for your life.

The deceiver will capitalize on every fear in your heart to convince you that God can't use you to redeem the world.

You can expect resistance from the enemy of your soul, and you can expect it from your flesh. Our temptation toward personal comforts, our natural draw to the pleasures of this world, creates resistance in us to God's radical call on our lives. So when you notice that resistance, don't be surprised. It's to be expected. When it comes, ask the Spirit to strengthen you to respond in obedience to God's voice and keep your eyes on Jesus. Expect to be strengthened.

Ask God to expose Satan's schemes that are keeping you from God's plan for your life.

3. Offer God Your Past

Expect the enemy to twist your past in an attempt to keep you from the beautiful plan God has for your life.

If you've been stuck in sin, yours or someone else's, the enemy will try to leverage that to discourage you. The deceiver will kindle shame in you, insisting that because of your past you are inadequate or disqualified from doing mighty things for God. The deceiver will also use the hardships you've faced—like illness or abuse or addiction or divorce—to distract and discourage you from living for God.

And yet there is nothing in your past that God cannot redeem.

In my life, Satan intended childhood cancer for evil. But through the unique circumstances of my life, God kindled in my heart a love for vulnerable children. Convincing me that every moment matters, God exposed the meaninglessness of so much of what the world values. And even in the disappointment of suffering a stroke that paralyzed my body, God taught me to depend on Him.

Friend, I have every confidence that God is in the business of redeeming all of your unique experiences— your hurts, your injuries, your disappointments—to mold you into the woman He created you to be. Nothing you've experienced in your lifetime is wasted, because God uses everything. In fact, He wants you to use your past hurts to rescue others going through them. No matter how big or small, ugly or painful, God will use what you've faced in your life for His glory.

If you're in the midst of suffering today, or if you're stuck in sin, you probably can't imagine how your life can be redeemed for good. But this is what God does! God takes what the enemy intended for evil and transforms you into the woman He designed you to be.

4. Protect Your Relationship with God

If we're to be a generation of women single-minded about God and His kingdom, we have to remove whatever hinders our relationship with Him. And that requires sacrifice.

Maybe God will invite you to release your Netflix subscription, social media accounts, or Monday night *Bachelor* watch party if any of those things are absorbing your time, energy, and imagination.

Maybe God will ask you to kick a habit—shopping online or going out on the weekends—to free you up to respond to Him.

And maybe God will ask you to end a relationship, friendship, or dating pattern that's toxic and steals your focus from what matters most.

I can't presume to know how God will ask you to cleanse your heart and mind. Sometimes the things God calls us to sacrifice are not bad things. Even some good things are stealing our time from the better plan. But I do believe that as you release all that's lifeless, you're set free to experience a more intimate relationship with the One who loves you.

Relationship with God is where you discover the purpose for your life.

The best way to protect your relationship with God looks a lot like what I had to do to stay healthy physically. I had to eat nutrient-rich foods. I had to follow my doctors' orders. I had to get enough rest. I had to avoid unnecessary dangers. I had to depend on the help and support of others. And that's exactly how to preserve a vibrant relationship with God. Feast on God's Word. Listen for God's voice in prayer. Make "God choices." Surround yourself with believers who share your commitment to pursue God with all your heart.

And if the Great Physician prescribes radical surgery— maybe excising something from your life that's killing you—show up for surgery early and accept every treatment prescribed.

5. Listen and Obey

God's faithful servants in the scriptures heard from God through prophets and teachers, priests and kings, voices and angels. Sometimes we can be tempted to believe that only happened "back then." But that kind of logic is simply a ploy by the enemy to dull our spiritual senses. God has not stopped speaking, and you and I can hear His voice today.

Sometimes God speaks to us through His Word.

Sometimes God speaks to us through mentors or committed Christian friends.

Sometimes God will put a phrase, or face, or place, or scripture passage on our hearts. Sometimes God speaks to us through an inspirational book.

I've learned that when we purpose to hear God's voice, when we soften our hearts and tip our eyes toward God's face, expecting to hear from Him, God is faithful. In fact, it is God's delight to communicate with us.

And we respond to God by obeying His voice.

If you ask Him to speak, be ready to obey!

Just as God called His leading world changers, like Moses, Mary, and Paul, God is still calling world changers today so that His kingdom can expand like wildfire to the ends of the earth! Though I believe that God's written Word, the Bible, is complete, I want to know that if God's next installment was written next year, my story would be in it! Not because of who I am, but because I believed God could do what He said He could do through me. I am convinced we have yet to see even greater miracles than Moses parting the sea.

The kingdom of God won't expand on this earth because we wish it to be so. God's kingdom reigns on earth as it reigns in heaven when God's people respond in obedience to His voice calling us to protect widows and orphans, feed the hungry, clothe the naked, visit the prisoner, and share the Gospel to the ends of the earth.

6. You Are God's Hands and God's Feet

Sister, the devil is at work in the world, and the people God is using to fight the enemy and build His kingdom are you and me.

Many of us have been distracted by our comforts and pleasures. Our insecurities and inadequacies. Our sin and shame. Until now we've been more concerned with the "likes" we accrue than with what moves God's heart. Our personal desire to make ourselves known has overshadowed our desire to make Christ known.

But in this moment, God is calling our generation to rise up and conquer the enemy. As we peel ourselves away from the fancy boutiques, cell phone screens, umbrella drinks, and designer boots, God is sending us into the world to be His light. He is waking us up from our slumber.

Paul exhorts, "For you were once darkness, but now you are light in the Lord. Live as children of light" (Ephesians 5:8). You are the mirror of light that God has chosen to bring light into the world.

Daily we are tempted away from the daring adventure of following God by the lure of stability, comfort, pleasure. We're promised that this is what will satisfy. But in the end, the pursuit of our own agenda is hollow, and we're left feeling lonely and dissatisfied. We've been made for so much more than comfort.

You were created to imitate the life of Jesus. That means you'll identify with the kind of people He spent time with. You'll challenge the assumptions He challenged. You'll share good news with the poor. You'll empty yourself for the sake of others. You'll access your resources and networks for the good of the kingdom.

God is at work around the world and in your life right now. It's not a coincidence that He is stirring your heart for something more. He wants to be close to you. He wants to use you and speak into your life.

Just as my story is unique, yours is, too. As a girl I never would have dreamed that I would fight cancer, open a business in college, fight for the lives of orphans, and send the Gospel to the ends of the earth. I don't know how your story will unfold, but I do believe that

God longs to write His story through you.

Precious sister, if you're like most of the women I know, you've searched for satisfaction someplace. Maybe it has been through your career. Your appearance. Your husband. Your child. But I want you to know there is so much more. God has a purpose for your life that involves His kingdom and His people. You will know deep and lasting joy and meaning as you pursue God's dream for your life.

There will come a day when the only thing that will matter is if you took Jesus seriously when He said He could use you to change the world. Today, you have the choice to say yes to God. You have the opportunity to release the dreams you've been clutching and exchange them for something so much better. If you're wavering about fully responding to God's plan over your own, your life might continue to look like a lot of the lives of the girls around you. But if you run hard after God, I promise that you are in for the adventure of your life.

Remember that there are lives waiting to be impacted on the other side of your obedience. You were made to accomplish God's dream for the world.

NOTES

1. Charel Schmit, "Facts and Numbers about Orphaned and Abandoned Children," ANCES, FICE Europe, 2006, http://www.ances.lu/index.php/fice/ fice-europa/25-facts-a-numbers-about-orphaned-and-abandoned-children; Michael Lipka and Conrad Hackett, "Why Muslims Are the World's Fastest-Growing Religious Group," Pew Research Center, April 6, 2017, http://www.pewresearch.org/ fact-tank/2017/04/06/why-muslims-are-the-worlds-fastest-growing-religious-group/.

2. Joy Dawson, *Forever Ruined for the Ordinary: The Adventure of Hearing and Obeying God's Voice* (Nashville: Thomas Nelson, 2001), 37, 71.

3. Pi James, "Learning to Be Leaders in Uganda," UNICEF, March 12, 2010, https://www.unicef.org/ infobycountry/uganda_53009.html.

4. Chelsea Evans, "Top 5 Facts about Poverty in Haiti," The Borgen Project, September 2015, https://borgen project.org/top-five-facts-about-poverty-in-haiti/.

DISCUSSION QUESTIONS

CHAPTER 1: THE DAY EVERYTHING CHANGES

Because our time on this earth is fleeting,
every moment matters.

- To what degree do you live with a daily awareness that your hours and minutes on this earth are fleeting? ("0" means you never give it a thought, and "10" means you think of nothing else.)
- Do you live differently today because you know your time on earth is temporary?
- Often when we pause to notice, we realize we already know those areas where we're spending—in big ways or small ones—our time, money, and energy (a.k.a. God's resources). Can you identify those areas in your life? What might God be asking you to release, or to "lose," to find your life?

Dream Challenge: The way you spend your moments matters. This week, start practicing ways to guard your time with the Lord by trading in something you value for something else you value even more. Give God one area of your life that you sense could be maximized for His glory. Netflix? Instagram? A coffee appointment? Yoga class? Write down your commitment to sacrifice one time-sucking activity from your week, as well as a practical way you can offer that time to God. (If you keep a journal, record the results!) Every minute matters!

Tip: Your "offering" could be one hour (during your favorite show?) or ten. What matters most is starting to spend your time and energy on things that are not fleeting.

CHAPTER 2:
ST. JUDE'S, WISHES, AND ENRIQUE IGLESIAS

Expect trials on the journey.

- What types of trials have you faced in the past or are facing now? (They don't have to be life-threatening. Trials come in all shapes and sizes.) Write them down in a journal.
- When you look at the current trials in your life, are you able to trust God when your future is not yet clear?
- What evidence do you see in scripture, and in the lives of others, that trials are part of the journey? If you squint through the pain, are you able to see what the Lord is waiting to teach you through this trial?

Dream Challenge: When Tiffany faced trials, she and her family turned their faces toward God. They prayed, they sang, and they affirmed that God's promises are bigger than their circumstances. Have you developed practices that knit your heart to God's when you suffer and when you face challenges that feel bigger than you? Perhaps a song about God's faithfulness has been a source of strength. Maybe a particular scripture verse carries you in difficult days. This week, choose a scripture or a song about one of God's promises to embrace and stand upon every day. Soon enough, you will know it by heart, remembering who is your source of strength!

Tip: Read or sing this promise every morning and allow the Lord to build your faith.

CHAPTER 3: THE DEVIL'S HAND

Satan attempts to thwart God's dream.

- If the enemy is the one who has come to steal, kill, and destroy, where have you seen his hand in your life in the past?
- Where do you recognize the grip of the evil one in your life today?
- As you think about where the enemy has a foothold in your life today, which part of the battle against Satan is yours to wage? And which part belongs to God?

Dream Challenge: Fighting the enemy and his tactics is always a holy combination of what God does and what we do. Pause to notice where the enemy is attacking you today. Is it your image? Financial troubles? Sickness? Shame? Past decisions? Sinful habits? Prayerfully offer this struggle to God, who fights for you, and ask Him to uproot any lies that are taking ground in your heart. Also choose one action you can take today to engage in the fight. Maybe you will text a friend to join you in prayer. Maybe you will read the Word, filling your mind with truth, or set greater boundaries between you and any sinful behaviors. Take one step today to destroy the enemy's schemes that are stealing God's plan from you.

Tip: Read Ephesians 6:10–18 about the armor of God. Compare the verses to your current battle, looking for areas where you can guard your life. Write them down.

CHAPTER 4: FIGHTING MY WAY BACK

Our focus on the body isn't God's priority.

- It's not uncommon in our image-obsessed society to focus on our appearance. Is there something about your physical appearance you wish you could change? What is it?
- In today's world, we spend more time comparing, critiquing, and caring for how we look on the outside than we do on the inside. If you are honest with yourself, what are some areas on your inside, who you are, that could use work?
- What are some ways this week that you can practice focusing on internal beauty over physical beauty, shifting your focus onto what truly matters to the Lord? (For example, monitor the images you feed your mind, choose not to dwell on your own external "flaws," study who God says you are.) List as many as possible.

Dream Challenge: When God created you, His work was flawless. The world's scheme is to convince you otherwise. Highlighting physical beauty over inner beauty creates an impossible standard we will never reach, leaving us grabbing at an image that doesn't lead to fulfillment. When God designed you, He had your soul in mind. His vision for His daughters is that they would be eager to improve who they are on the inside: their character, their hearts, their souls. As you continue to think about the kind of woman God designed you to be, write down all the truths about who God has called you to be.

Tip: Acknowledge the areas of your body about which the enemy is discouraging you and ask the Lord to teach you to dwell on truth by seeking His Word. (A good starting point: Ephesians 2:10; 4:24; Proverbs 31.)

CHAPTER 5: WHAT A GIRL WANTS

God's dream is different than our plans.

- What if you could author a storybook life for yourself? What would that look like?
- Write down your full life dream. All the details! What have you done to work toward the fulfillment of that dream? How have you invested time, money, and energy into producing that story?
- Which parts of your story have matched your plan, and which ones have veered from the script you'd write?

Dream Challenge: Sometimes the story we hope to live is snatched from our grasp. When this happens—through illness, injury, broken relationships—we have very little power to change the trajectory of our stories. Other times we have more agency over the arc of our stories. Make a list of the key markers of the story you planned for your life: education, career, marriage, parenthood, service, wealth, home, etc. Try to come up with five to ten markers of the story you once imagined for your life. Let this list become your prayer guide over the next month. Each day, offer these hopes and plans to God with an open hand, inviting Him to write His story in your life.

Tip: Philippians 2:7 says that Jesus "emptied himself" or "made himself nothing." This month, empty yourself before God, inviting His will to be done in your life.

CHAPTER 6:
EIGHTEEN WEDDINGS AND ONE NEW LOVE

Comparing yourself and your story to others is deadly.

- It can be tempting to compare ourselves to others by tipping our eyes toward those who seem successful, have a certain image, have been given different opportunities, or are at different stages of life than us. As you consider the different seasons of your life, who are some of those faces you've turned to?
- It has been said that comparison is the thief of joy. Is there a certain area in which you tend to compare yourself to others?
- Have you noticed women who have little interest in comparing themselves to others? Name some women you know who reflect this kind of confidence.

Dream Challenge: Is it easy or difficult for you to believe that you are unique in all the world? Because God's plan for your life is different from His plan for anyone else's life, God has designed you like no other. Though it's tempting to want to be like others, you honor God by noticing and embracing what makes your story so special! Comparison leads to competition, which ultimately leads to discontent. You honor God by becoming the woman He made you to be. Because you have a calling on your life that only you can fulfill with the skills you possess at this very moment in history, embracing your differences is crucial! Begin a list of talents, passions, gifts, and characteristics that are unique to you. Whether it's an artistic ability, an outgoing personality, a heart for evangelism, a fiery passion for justice, or perfect pitch, list everything that makes you who you are, and offer those qualities to God.

Tip: When you notice yourself comparing your life to someone else's, pause to redirect your mind to the calling God has ahead of you!

CHAPTER 7: WHEN GOD SPEAKS

God invites us to walk out His plan with others.

- Have you ever heard God speak to you? If so, in what ways? Through scripture, through hearing, through signs and wonders?
- Is there something God keeps putting on your heart but you haven't stepped out in faith to see it come to pass? What is it?
- What are the questions on your heart that you would like God to answer?

Dream Challenge: God is alive and active; He delights in speaking to His children and telling them the mysteries of their hearts. If you are looking for direction, purpose, your next step, or answers to questions that have been on your heart, listen closely! You probably won't hear Him speak if you aren't actively listening. Take time to get alone and be quiet and still before the Lord. Ask Him to silence all voices that aren't Him and to speak to you so that you may experience His power. Ask Him to show you how He wants to use you. And then listen. Stay quiet and listen. It may be a few days or weeks before He speaks, but be continuously aware that He will speak!

Tip: God speaks clearly through His Word.

CHAPTER 8: MY COMFORTS EXPOSED

God exposes our privilege to move us to respond to pain.

- Have you taken time to stop and ask the Lord to allow you to see through His eyes? How might He want you to use your story to change the story of others?
- Is there any group of people in particular He has put on your heart?
- If being a "follower of Christ" means following Christ, what are some areas where you struggle to follow His lead?

Dream Challenge: As God begins to grip our hearts, transforming them to care about the things He cares about, He wants to expose the areas of this world that break His heart. He wants us to follow His lead in rescuing a lost world. One way to better understand Jesus is to study His life. Read one of the Gospels—Matthew, Mark, Luke, or John—and using your journal, take note of the way Jesus lived His life: whom He hung out with, what He said, what He sacrificed.

Tip: By studying the life of Jesus, you stay close to His heart for those in need.

CHAPTER 9: ORPHAN RAVE

God calls you to serve Him where you are.

- Mother Teresa said we can't do great things, only small things with great love. Do any small things you're doing now align with your sense of God's calling to build His kingdom?
- Sometimes the Spirit nudges us to engage, but we ignore God's gentle leading. Is there something, today, that you've heard from God but have been slow to respond to?
- Is anyone near you—a friend, a ministry leader, someone at church—living out the kind of calling you're sensing from God? Can you join them?

Dream Challenge: Many of us want to believe that if God came to us in a mysterious, mighty form—as He addressed the boy Samuel in the temple or as He spoke to Mary through Gabriel—we'd be quick to say yes. And we can even fool ourselves, as we lead mediocre lives, to believe that we would. But the scriptural witness, as well as modern Christians following Him today, shows that more often than not, God works with those who are already in the habit of saying yes. That means we are constantly preparing our hearts for the big "yes"—to quit our jobs, or relocate, or adopt, or sell our belongings—with smaller "yeses": to read, to pray, to serve, to love. Today, what is one small "yes" that God is waiting to hear from you?

Tip: Spending time alone with God in prayer and His Word is the best place to start offering your small yeses.

CHAPTER 10: EVERY YES MATTERS

God uses our yes to bring life out of death.

- When you examine your own life, actions, and ways you use your time, money, and energy, are you quicker to say no or yes?
- Are there any current habits, trials, or struggles in your life that feel deadly to you? In what ways can God bring life into these struggles?
- What would God need to do in your life to inspire or equip you to say yes to His call?

Dream Challenge: Through Christ's life, death, and resurrection, God delivers all of humanity from our sin, sorrow, and shame. God longs for every person to have a transforming relationship with Him, and we are the ones God uses to invite others into His family. Are you passionate about helping others come to know Jesus? Do you feel that sharing the Gospel is work for others, but not you? Pray and ask God to give you His heart for lost souls. Ask God to cultivate in your heart the desire to say yes to what He has planned for you.

Tip: Start a prayer log to track your prayers and moments you choose to say yes. As you pray, you'll be able to look back and see God answering your prayers in His perfect timing.

CHAPTER 11: OUT OF EXCUSES

*God asks us to sacrifice both our
comfort and our resistance.*

- Think back to something you promised you'd never do for God. What was it? If you have never made a vow like that, what might you have been likely to resist?
- Let's say God invites you to do that thing you promised you'd never do. Maybe it's going to another country. Maybe it's remaining single for a season. Maybe it's forfeiting earthly comfort. Maybe something else. What would you gain by refusing God's invitation? What would you lose?
- Who do you know who has followed God's hard calling on their life? Who said yes when it wasn't comfortable?

Dream Challenge: When we think about responding to God's call, it can be exciting to imagine using the unique gifts, talents, and skills God has given us. But when God's call disrupts our comfort or triggers our fears, it can be less appealing. We may be tempted to respond to God's call halfheartedly. God, though, wants us to trust Him with everything. I promise you, it's worth it. This week, practice praying three words: "God, I'm willing." Let God know you're willing to sacrifice whatever it takes to say yes to His leading. This takes courage, friend! But you won't be sorry.

Tip: Practice a posture of openness to God's leading by simply praying "yes" to God throughout your day.

CHAPTER 12: BONDYE NOU AU GRAN

God is passionate about saving souls through the Gospel.

- On their trip to Haiti, Tiffany's team had the opportunity to meet people's physical needs and also share the Gospel of Christ with those who desperately needed to hear it. Which of those two expressions of love comes most naturally to you? Which is more difficult? Why?
- What has been the most natural, authentic, and effective way for you to share the Gospel with others? For example, do you lead by sharing what Jesus has done in your life, or what Jesus has done for others? Describe one encounter God provided for you to share good news with others.
- What would God need to do in your life to inspire or equip you to share the hope of salvation with others?

Dream Challenge: You don't have to travel to a remote village in Haiti to share the Gospel with the world God loves. God's Spirit will quicken your heart and mind to notice and reach out to those in your life today. Make a list, in your journal or on a Post-it note you can post in your room, of the family, friends, neighbors, and coworkers in your current orbit who don't know Jesus. Pray over that list and ask God's Spirit to lead you to share with one of those people. Continue to commit that person to prayer.

Tip: You don't have to have special giftings to share the Gospel. When you respond to God by sharing Christ with others, the Spirit equips you with all the love, wisdom, and grace you need.

CHAPTER 13: LIFE INTERRUPTED

God interrupts our plans for the sake of His.

- How do you react when your plans are interrupted—by someone's sudden urgent need, by a devastating trial, or by something else out of your control?
- Sometimes we can make an idol of our plans—the career we'll build, the home we'll own, the family we imagine. Which part of your plan is the hardest to trust God with?
- Are there ways in which you've already seen your plan for your life change course? How have you handled those detours?

Dream Challenge: Many of God's people in scripture had their plans interrupted. In fact, when God called His faithful ones to a special assignment, interrupted plans seem to have been the rule and not the exception! Make a list of as many people in scripture as you can think of who had their lives interrupted by God. In one column, describe the life they'd been living. In a second column, describe the adventure into which God called them. Then prayerfully offer yourself to be used by God.

Tip: Pray this week, "God, I welcome You to interrupt my plans with Your dream."

CHAPTER 14: MOTHER OF MANY

God asks us to release our dreams for the sake of His.

- Had Yvrose clung to her dream, what would be different about her life today? And what would be different about Haiti?
- Had Tiffany clung to her dream, what would be different about her life today? And what would be different for those in places where she has worked?
- Today, what is your dream? If you refuse to hold it lightly, what might your life look like in ten years?

Dream Challenge: When she sought God's will for her life, Tiffany was given the word *orphans* from God. Five years later, though, God birthed in her heart a dream for the Gospel to reach those who don't yet know Christ. Like swinging on monkey bars, she had to be willing to grab the next bar! Ask God what you've been holding on to—it could be your dream, or it could even be God's plan for an earlier season—that you need to release in order to step into God's current dream for your life. Even if you can't yet see the new, write down the old and offer it to God. (If you're feeling crazy, drop it in a metal trash can and light it on fire!)

Tip: Sometimes God invites us to release something that's not a bad thing so that we can grasp something even better.

CHAPTER 15: WHAT GOD CAN DO

God uses His people to execute His plans.

- Because Yvrose and Pierre Richard said yes, God rescued and redeemed thirty-four children. What is God accomplishing through your smaller yeses?
- God used one man with a big prayer to change a community in Haiti. What is the big prayer on your heart?
- God gave Jeanathon and Tiffany the same dream. Do you know anyone who shares the God-dream that is in your heart?

Dream Challenge: There aren't a lot of ways God redeems the world. In fact, there's just one! God took on human flesh to redeem the world through Jesus, and today the human agents God chooses to use are the followers who pattern their lives after Him. Yvrose and those in her community prayed big prayers. Are you willing to join them? This week, write down one big prayer in your journal, and continue to seek God for that big thing. It might take three days. It might take three years. If your request conforms to God's heart, stick with it!

Tip: Think big! You can trust that God has access to all the resources you need to accomplish what He's called you to do.

CHAPTER 16: EMBRACING YOUR PURPOSE

God has a good plan for you.

- Compare your dream from chapter 5 to the greater
- plan the Lord is revealing to you. Are there any similarities?
- What are the differences?
- Does the way you live your life reveal that you are more consumed by the approval of your Leader than of your followers, or vice versa? How so?

Dream Challenge: God wants nothing more than to speak His plan for your life to your heart. If you're not in the habit of listening, here is your opportunity! Crack open a new journal for the adventure and choose a period of time when you will devote yourself to listening for God's voice. (Ideally, you're always listening, but committing three months, or six months, to disciplined listening is a solid investment.) Share your plan with a mentor or friend who can pray alongside you during this time. Read widely in the scriptures—Old Testament and New, Moses and Jesus, Psalms and Ephesians, etc.—and ask God to guide you. Record what you're hearing and learning—through scripture, through prayer, through trusted individuals who love you and love God. Most importantly, act. Take a step in faith in the direction God is opening your eyes to. That step might be as simple as writing a check, reading a book, or volunteering locally. Your willingness to obey opens doors for God to keep speaking to your heart and directing you toward His greatest calling, growing His kingdom.

Tip: When you respond in obedience to God's voice, you keep your heart soft and ready to receive your next instruction. Get ready to live your life for something greater than yourself!